D1424668

C333201149

SALARIYA

© The Salariya Book Company Ltd MMXIII
All rights reserved. No part of this book may be
reproduced, stored in a retrieval system or transmitted in
any form or by any means, electronic, mechanical,
photocopying, recording or otherwise, without the written
permission of the copyright owner.

Published in Great Britain in MMXIII by
Book House, an imprint of
The Salariya Book Company Ltd
25 Marlborough Place, Brighton BN1 1UB

1 3 5 7 9 8 6 4 2

Please visit our website at **www.salariya.com**
for **free** electronic versions of:
You Wouldn't Want to Be an Egyptian Mummy!
You Wouldn't Want to Be a Roman Gladiator!
You Wouldn't Want to be a Polar Explorer!
You Wouldn't Want to sail on a 19th-Century Whaling Ship!

Authors:
Mark Bergin was born in Hastings, England, in 1961.
He studied at Eastbourne College of Art and has
specialised in historical reconstructions as well as aviation
and maritime subjects since 1983. He lives in
Bexhill-on-Sea with his wife and three children.

David Antram was born in Brighton, England, in 1958. He
studied at Eastbourne College of Art and then worked in
advertising for fifteen years before becoming a full-time artist.
He has illustrated many children's non-fiction books.

Editor: Rob Walker

PB ISBN: 978-1-908759-68-9

A CIP catalogue record for this
book is available from the
British Library.

Printed and bound in China.
Printed on paper from
sustainable sources.

PAPER FROM
SUSTAINABLE
FORESTS

**WARNING: Fixatives should be
used only under adult supervision.**

You Tube
@bookhousebooks   The Salariya   BookHouse100
                  Book Company

FIND OUR BOOKS
ON THE APP STORE:
SEARCH FOR 'SALARIYA'

Visit our **new** online shop at
shop.salariya.com
for great offers, gift ideas, all our new releases
and free postage and packaging.

DRAW

THINGS THAT GO

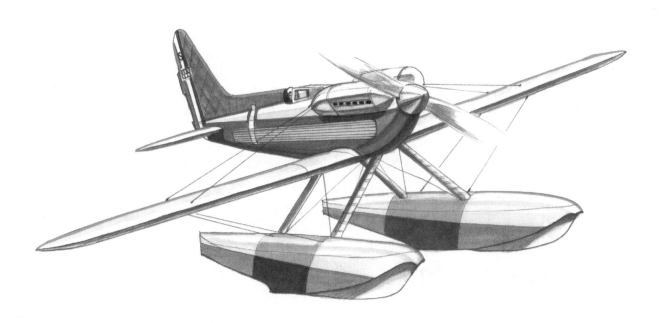

BOOK HOUSE HOUSE

Contents

6 Drawing materials

8 Perspective

10 Honda Civic R

12 Aston Martin DBS

14 Ford GT

16 Subaru Impreza

18 NASCAR

20 Bentley Speed 8

22 Ferrari FXX

24 Ferrari F1

26 Thrust SSC

28 Fokker DR1 Triplane

30 Supermarine Spitfire

32 Supermarine S6B

34 Pitts Special

36 'Blackbird'

38 Concorde

40 F—16A Fighting Falcon

42 Airbus A380

44 Space Ship One

46 Speedboat

48 Racing yacht

50 Rowing boat

52 Topsail schooner

54 Ocean tanker

56 Fishing boat

58 Ocean liner

60 Pirate ship

62 Fire engine

64 Articulated truck

66 Racing truck

68 Snow plough

70 Tanker

72 Future truck

74 Giant dump truck

76 Monster truck

78 Freestyle BMX

80 Skateboarding

82 River rafting

84 ATV racing

86 Wheels

88 Wakeboarding

90 Spacecraft

92 Space vehicles

94 Glossary and index

Drawing materials

DRAW

Try using different types of drawing papers and materials. Experiment with charcoal, wax crayons and pastels. All pens, from felt–tips to ballpoints will make interesting marks, or try drawing with pen and ink on wet paper.

Hard **pencils** are greyer and soft pencils are blacker. Hard pencils are graded from 6H (the hardest) through 5H, 4H, 3H, 2H to H. Soft pencils are graded from B through 1B, 2B, 3B, 4B, 5B up to 6B (the softest).

Charcoal is very soft and can be used for big, bold drawings. Spray charcoal drawings with fixative* to prevent further smudging (see page 2).

Pastels are even softer than charcoal, and come in a wide range of colours. Spray pastel drawings with fixative* too, to prevent further smudging (see page 2).

Silhouette

Create special effects by scraping away parts of a drawing done with **wax crayons**.

Lines drawn in ink cannot be erased so keep your ink drawings sketchy and less rigid. Don't worry about mistakes as these can be lost in the drawing as it develops.

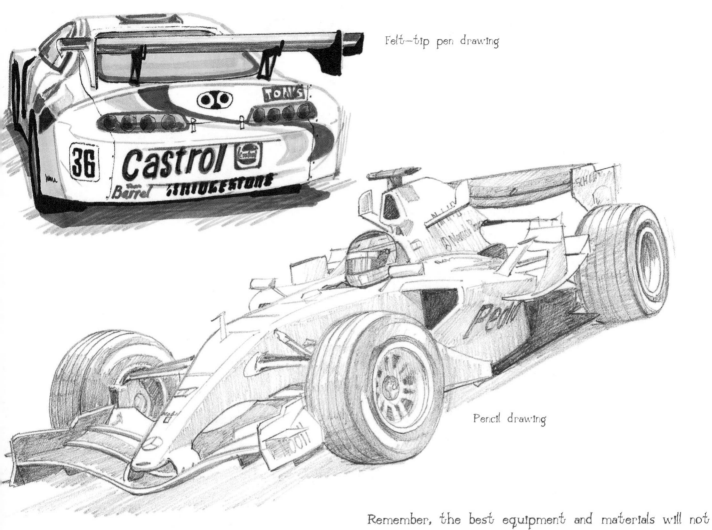

Felt-tip pen drawing

Pencil drawing

Remember, the best equipment and materials will not necessarily make the best drawing — practice will!

Line pen drawing

Perspective DRAW

If you look at a car from different viewpoints, you will see that the part of the car that is closest to you will look larger, and the part furthest away from you will look smaller. Drawing in perspective is a way of creating a feeling of space and three dimensions on a flat surface.

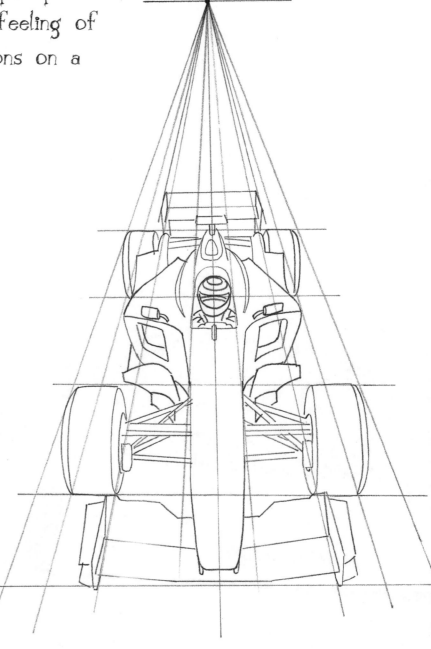

(Below) A single high vanishing point. From this viewpoint a car looks as if it is zooming out towards you.

V.P.

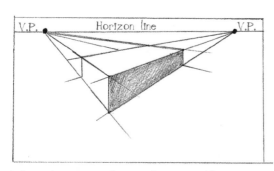

(Above) A car's basic shape is like a rectangular box. Most car drawings can start with this type of shape.

(Right) Note how the construction lines get wider apart as they get closer to you. Towards the back of the car, the lines are closer together because it is further away from you.

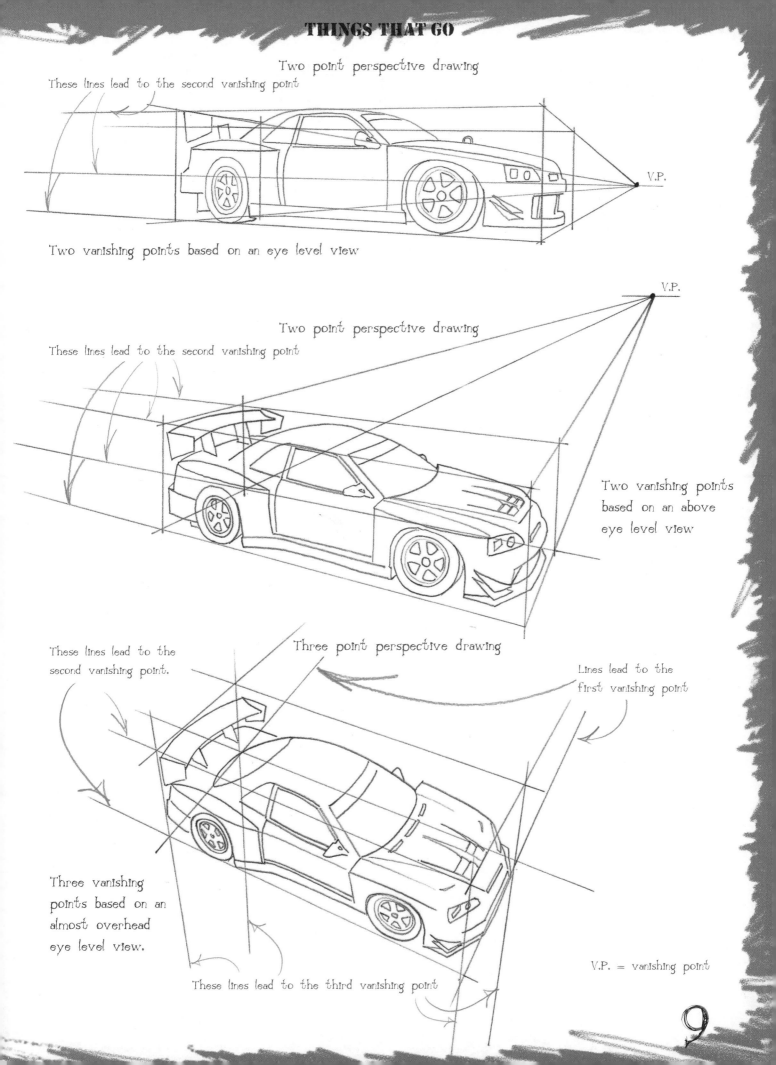

Two point perspective drawing

These lines lead to the second vanishing point

V.P.

Two vanishing points based on an eye level view

Two point perspective drawing

These lines lead to the second vanishing point

V.P.

Two vanishing points based on an above eye level view

Three point perspective drawing

These lines lead to the second vanishing point.

Lines lead to the first vanishing point

Three vanishing points based on an almost overhead eye level view.

These lines lead to the third vanishing point

V.P. = vanishing point

9

Honda Civic R

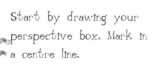

The Honda Civic R can be customised to a driver's specifications. The addition of chrome wheels, air intakes, skirt and a powerful turbo engine can transform this car into an urban street racer.

Start by drawing your perspective box. Mark in a centre line.

Be careful when drawing the wheel ellipses.

The front wheel is turning — so it is at a different angle from the back wheel.

Centre line

Now draw the main body using the centre line for the three-dimensional shape.

Ink

Draw simple curved lines for the bodywork.

Pointed front end.

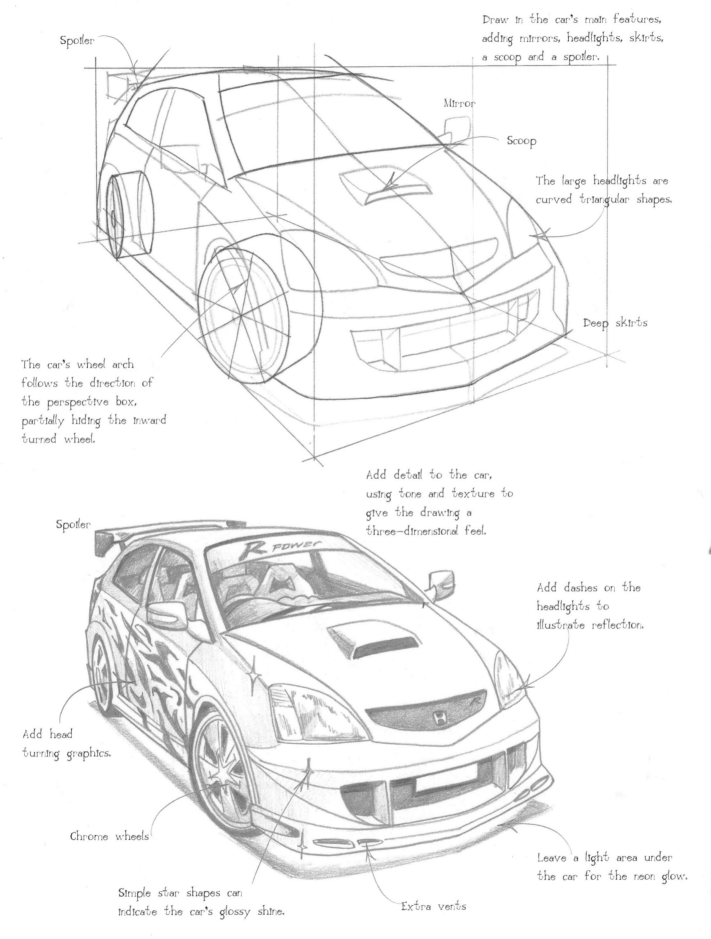

Draw in the car's main features, adding mirrors, headlights, skirts, a scoop and a spoiler.

Spoiler

Mirror

Scoop

The large headlights are curved triangular shapes.

Deep skirts

The car's wheel arch follows the direction of the perspective box, partially hiding the inward turned wheel.

Add detail to the car, using tone and texture to give the drawing a three-dimensional feel.

Spoiler

R power

Add dashes on the headlights to illustrate reflection.

Add head turning graphics.

Chrome wheels

Leave a light area under the car for the neon glow.

Simple star shapes can indicate the car's glossy shine.

Extra vents

DRAW
Aston Martin DBS

The Aston Martin DBS is James Bond's car in the 2006 film 'Casino Royale'. Its style and power have made it a new British classic.

Start by drawing a simple perspective box with a centre line.

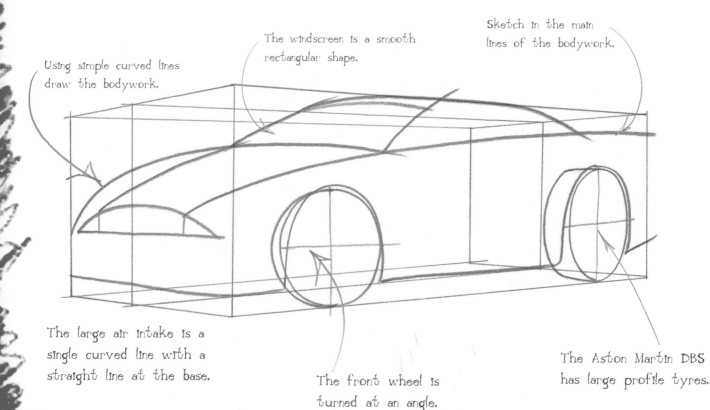

Using simple curved lines draw the bodywork.

The windscreen is a smooth rectangular shape.

Sketch in the main lines of the bodywork.

The large air intake is a single curved line with a straight line at the base.

The front wheel is turned at an angle.

The Aston Martin DBS has large profile tyres.

Use different shapes to frame your composition. This can improve your drawing.

Draw in the main features of the car, adding mirrors, windows, headlights, doors and skirts.

Draw the air intake in the skirts using straight lines.

Add lines for the door, note how they curve in at the top to follow the shape of the bodywork.

Draw in the small rear end of the car using a series of curved lines.

Don't forget to draw in parts like the door pillar on the far side.

Now add the final details to the car.

Darken areas where the light would not reach.

Divide the wheel into triangular sections and add detail for the large alloy wheels.

Add tone to the bodywork to give it a three-dimensional look.

13

Ford GT *DRAW*

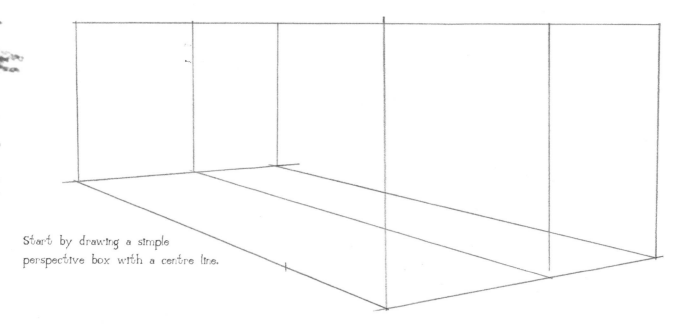

The Ford GT is a redesigned version of the 1960s classic Le Mans winning car, the GT40. This 2002 American car is longer and larger than the GT40 and has a supercharged V8 engine.

Start by drawing a simple perspective box with a centre line.

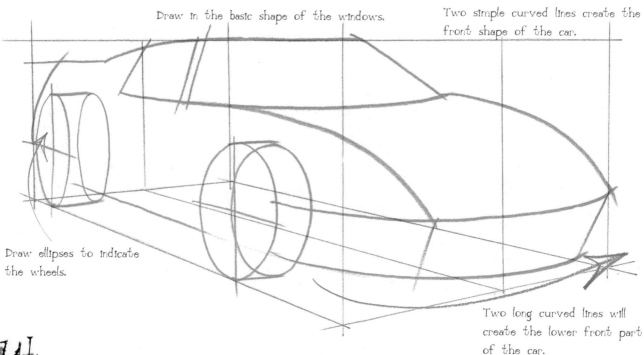

Draw in the basic shape of the windows.

Two simple curved lines create the front shape of the car.

Draw ellipses to indicate the wheels.

Two long curved lines will create the lower front part of the car.

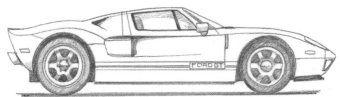

Add the main features of the car: air intakes, headlights and side mirrors.

You can use profile drawings or photographs to help you with size and proportion. They can be a great help for the detail of wheels and air intakes.

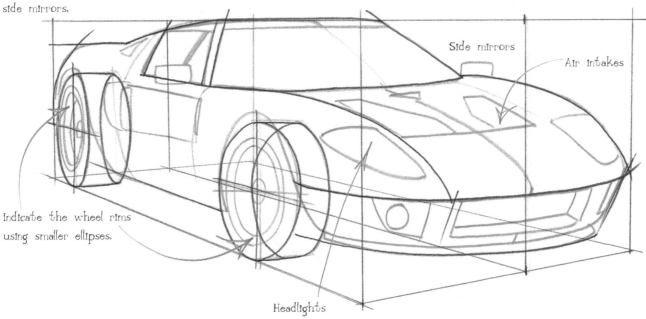

Side mirrors

Air intakes

Indicate the wheel rims using smaller ellipses.

Headlights

To create highlights on the shining bodywork you must leave these areas of your paper white.

Window reflections need to be left white too.

Darken areas of your drawing where the light would not reach.

Remove any construction lines.

Add the Ford double stripes.

Draw Subaru Impreza

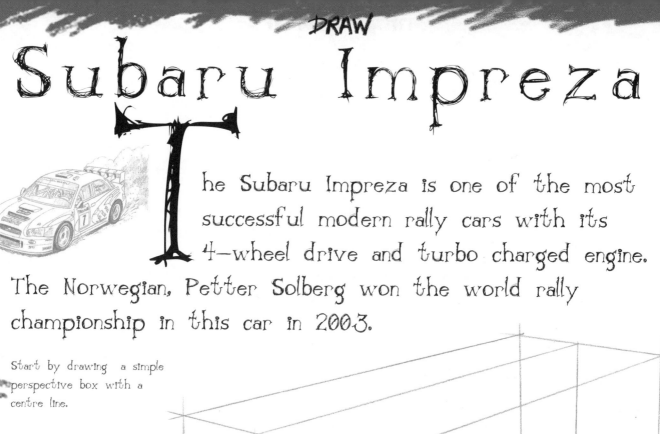

The Subaru Impreza is one of the most successful modern rally cars with its 4-wheel drive and turbo charged engine. The Norwegian, Petter Solberg won the world rally championship in this car in 2003.

Start by drawing a simple perspective box with a centre line.

Sketch in the wheels with ellipses.

Draw in a simple rectangular shape for the windscreen and the roof.

Add the car's basic body shape.

Use curved lines to draw in the front of the car.

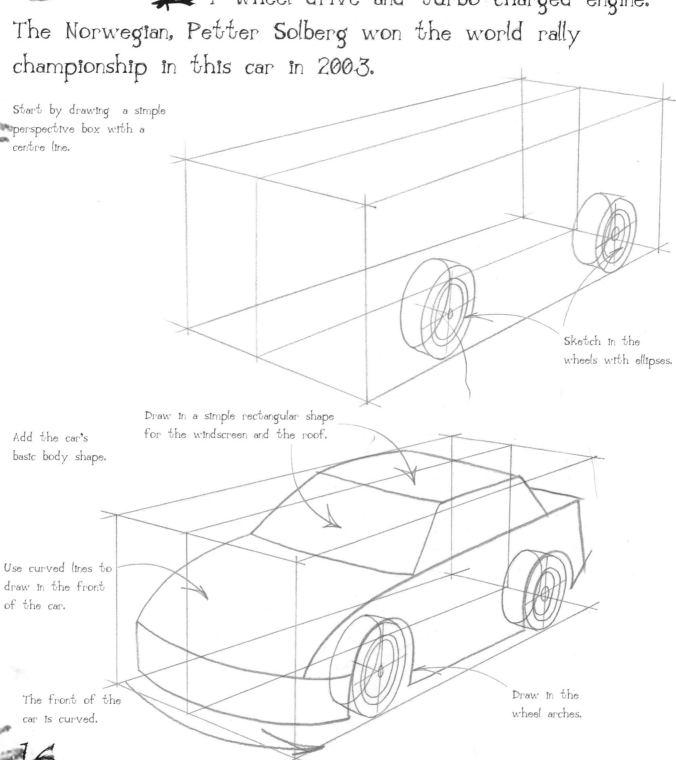

The front of the car is curved.

Draw in the wheel arches.

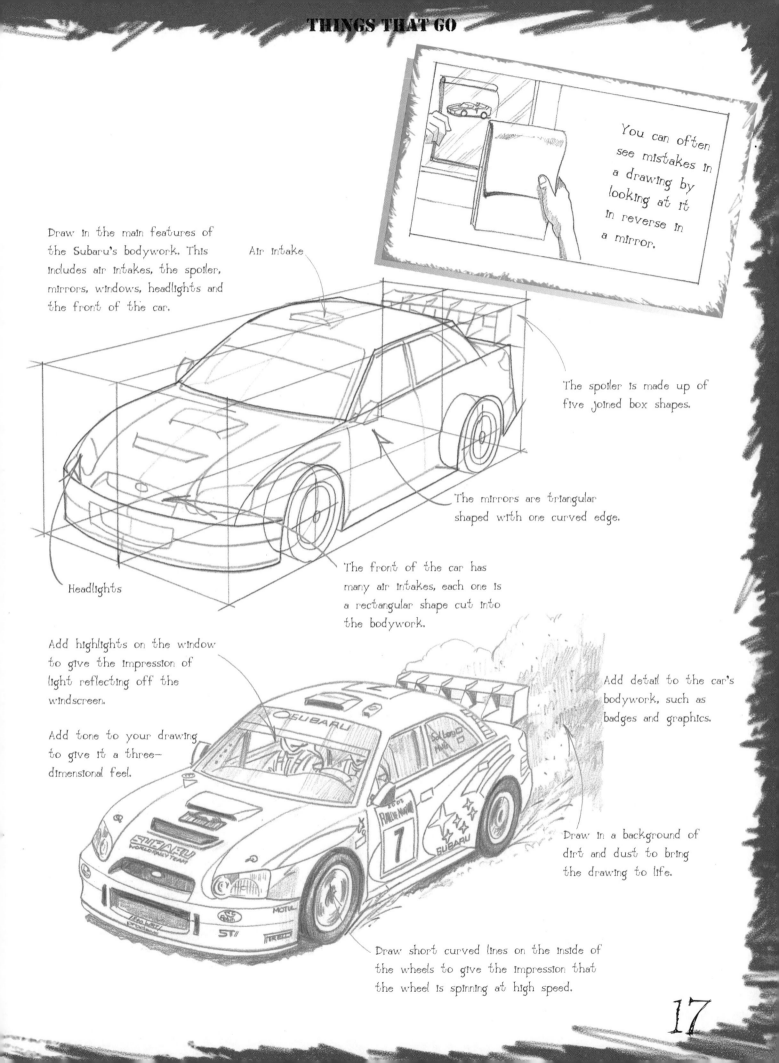

You can often see mistakes in a drawing by looking at it in reverse in a mirror.

Draw in the main features of the Subaru's bodywork. This includes air intakes, the spoiler, mirrors, windows, headlights and the front of the car.

Air intake

The spoiler is made up of five joined box shapes.

The mirrors are triangular shaped with one curved edge.

The front of the car has many air intakes, each one is a rectangular shape cut into the bodywork.

Headlights

Add highlights on the window to give the impression of light reflecting off the windscreen.

Add tone to your drawing to give it a three-dimensional feel.

Add detail to the car's bodywork, such as badges and graphics.

Draw in a background of dirt and dust to bring the drawing to life.

Draw short curved lines on the inside of the wheels to give the impression that the wheel is spinning at high speed.

17

NASCAR

NASCAR (National Association for Stock Car Auto Racing) in the USA races cars on oval circuits like Daytona. Its banked corners make it one of the most exciting and colourful experiences in motor-sport. Cars can average speeds of 320km/h as they pass close to one another.

Start your drawing with a simple perspective box with a centre line.

Draw in ellipses to indicate the position of the wheels.

Draw in the main bodywork.

Simple rectangular shapes can be used to draw the front windscreen and the roof.

The car bonnet is very long, use long curved lines to draw it.

The rear of the car is quite angular so use straight lines to draw it.

The main features of the car can now be added.

The windscreen is divided into three parts.

The rear spoiler is an upright rectangular shape.

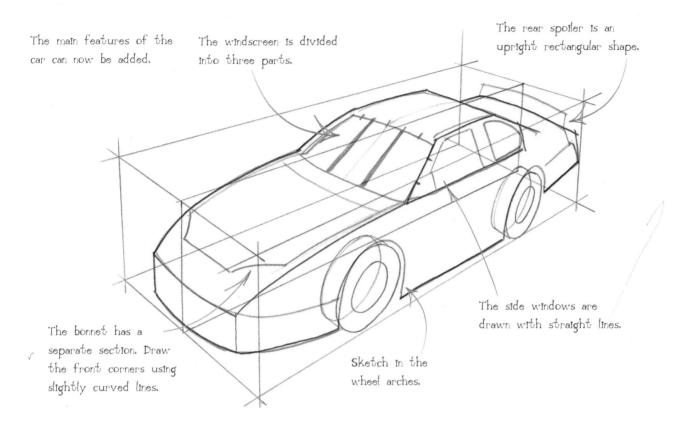

The bonnet has a separate section. Draw the front corners using slightly curved lines.

Sketch in the wheel arches.

The side windows are drawn with straight lines.

Now finish off the remaining features, the headlights, wheels and air intakes.

Make your car look like the real thing. Add lots of graphics and large race numbers which are easily seen from the stands.

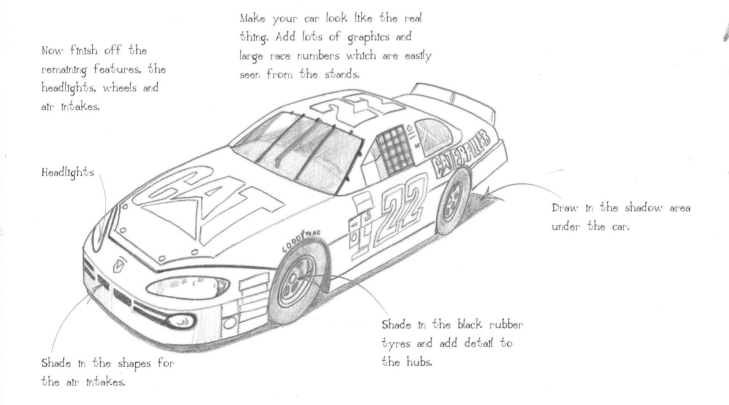

Headlights

Draw in the shadow area under the car.

Shade in the shapes for the air intakes.

Shade in the black rubber tyres and add detail to the hubs.

Bentley Speed 8

DRAW

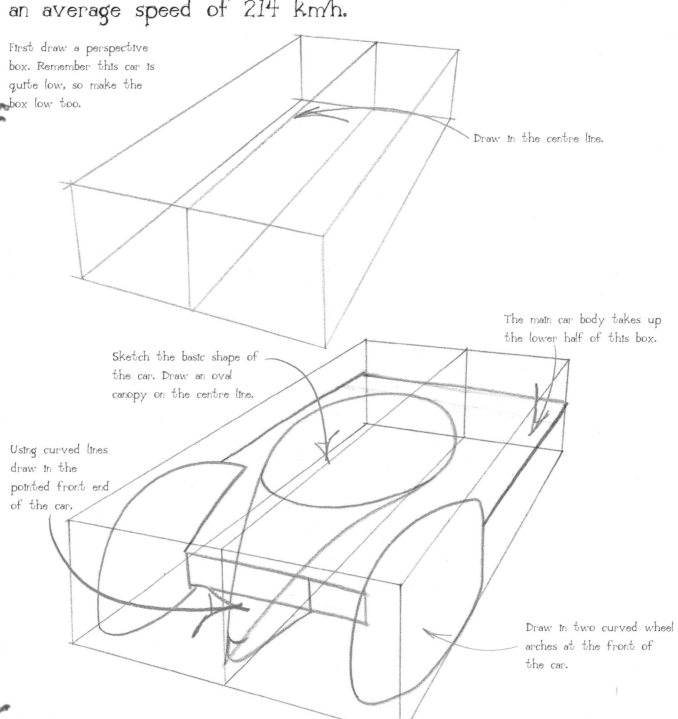

The Bentley Speed 8 won the Le Mans 24 Hour race in 2003. It covered 376 laps in this event — a distance of 5,145 km at an average speed of 214 km/h.

First draw a perspective box. Remember this car is quite low, so make the box low too.

Draw in the centre line.

The main car body takes up the lower half of this box.

Sketch the basic shape of the car. Draw an oval canopy on the centre line.

Using curved lines draw in the pointed front end of the car.

Draw in two curved wheel arches at the front of the car.

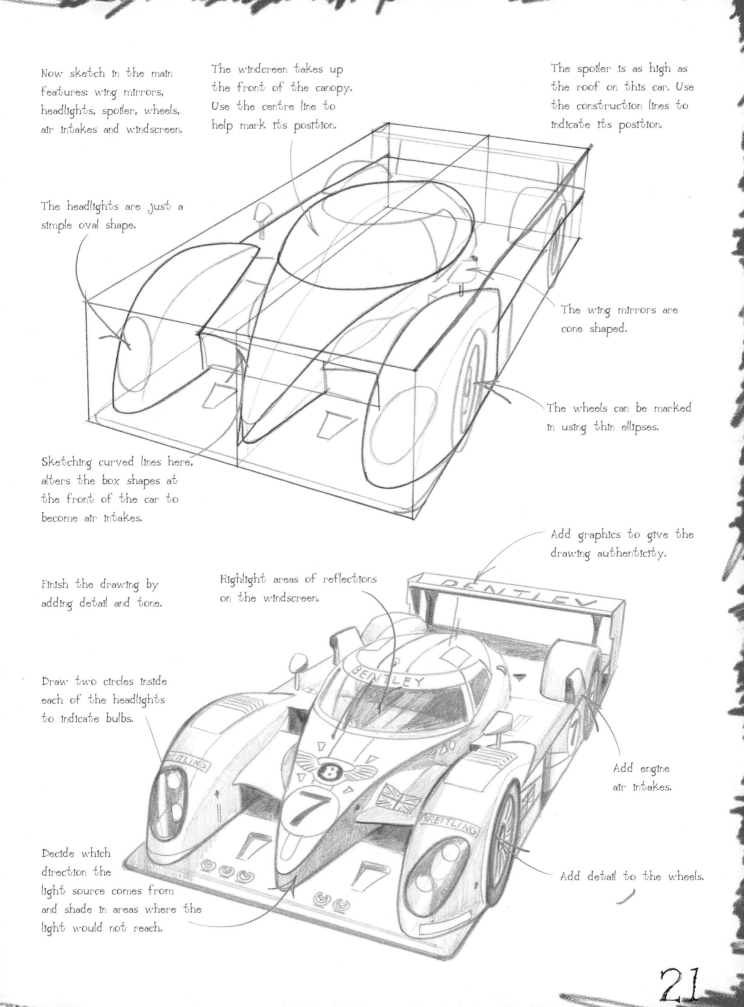

Now sketch in the main features: wing mirrors, headlights, spoiler, wheels, air intakes and windscreen.

The windcreen takes up the front of the canopy. Use the centre line to help mark its position.

The spoiler is as high as the roof on this car. Use the construction lines to indicate its position.

The headlights are just a simple oval shape.

The wing mirrors are cone shaped.

Sketching curved lines here, alters the box shapes at the front of the car to become air intakes.

The wheels can be marked in using thin ellipses.

Add graphics to give the drawing authenticity.

Finish the drawing by adding detail and tone.

Highlight areas of reflections on the windscreen.

Draw two circles inside each of the headlights to indicate bulbs.

Add engine air intakes.

Decide which direction the light source comes from and shade in areas where the light would not reach.

Add detail to the wheels.

21

Ferrari DRAW FXX

The Ferrari FXX is the latest Italian supercar. It is a Ferrari Enzo that has been tuned up and reworked to make it the ultimate track—day car. An **800** bhp engine propels this super light car (1155 kg) to a speed of almost 320 km/h!

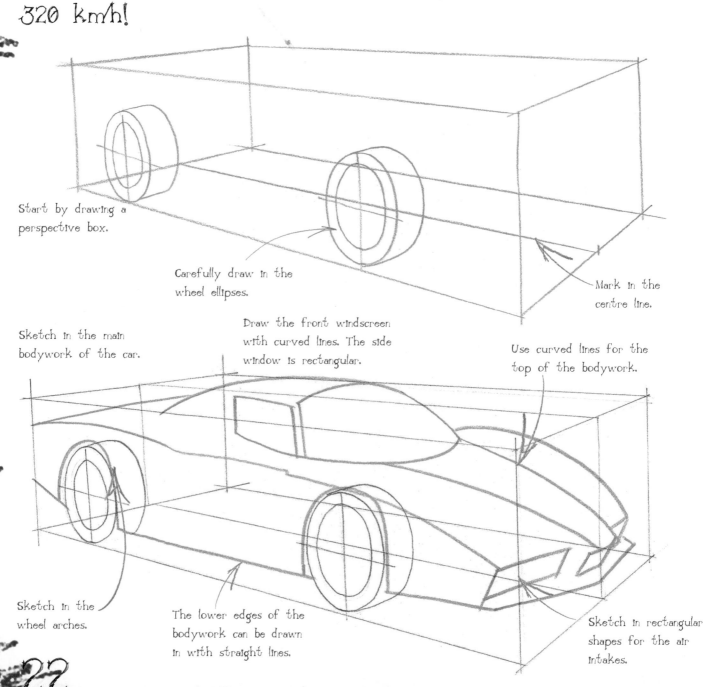

Start by drawing a perspective box.

Carefully draw in the wheel ellipses.

Mark in the centre line.

Sketch in the main bodywork of the car.

Draw the front windscreen with curved lines. The side window is rectangular.

Use curved lines for the top of the bodywork.

Sketch in the wheel arches.

The lower edges of the bodywork can be drawn in with straight lines.

Sketch in rectangular shapes for the air intakes.

Now add the main features of the Ferrari's bodywork.

The Ferrari's spoiler is quite complex. Construct it carefully using straight and curved lines.

Add the windscreeen wiper.

Sketch in the headlights.

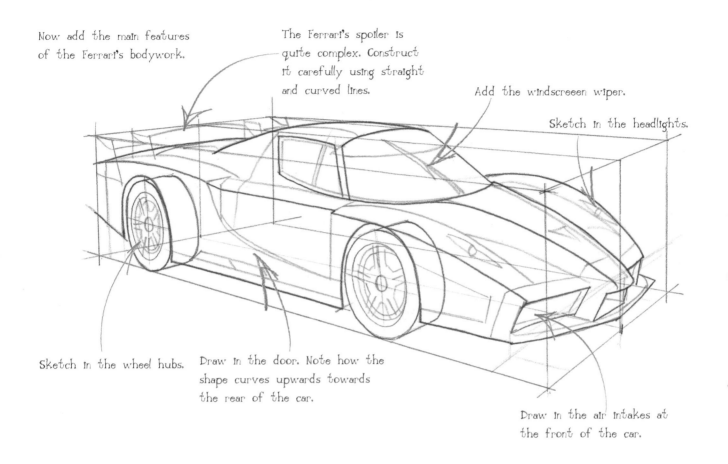

Sketch in the wheel hubs.

Draw in the door. Note how the shape curves upwards towards the rear of the car.

Draw in the air intakes at the front of the car.

Complete the drawing with these finishing touches.

Draw the letters 'FXX' onto the spoiler.

Add tone to the drawing, create highlights and shaded areas according to how the light falls on the car.

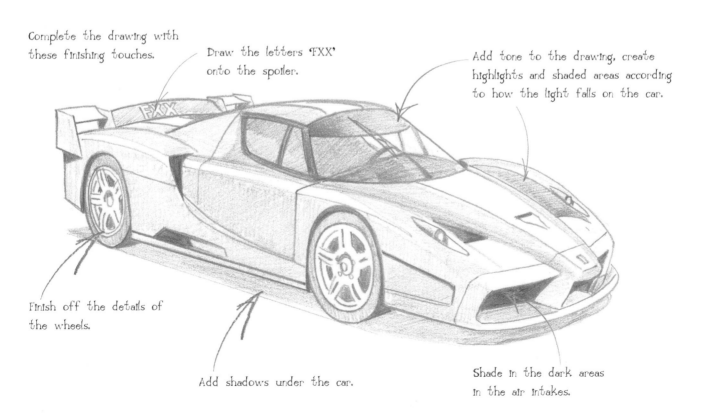

Finish off the details of the wheels.

Add shadows under the car.

Shade in the dark areas in the air intakes.

Ferrari F1
DRAW

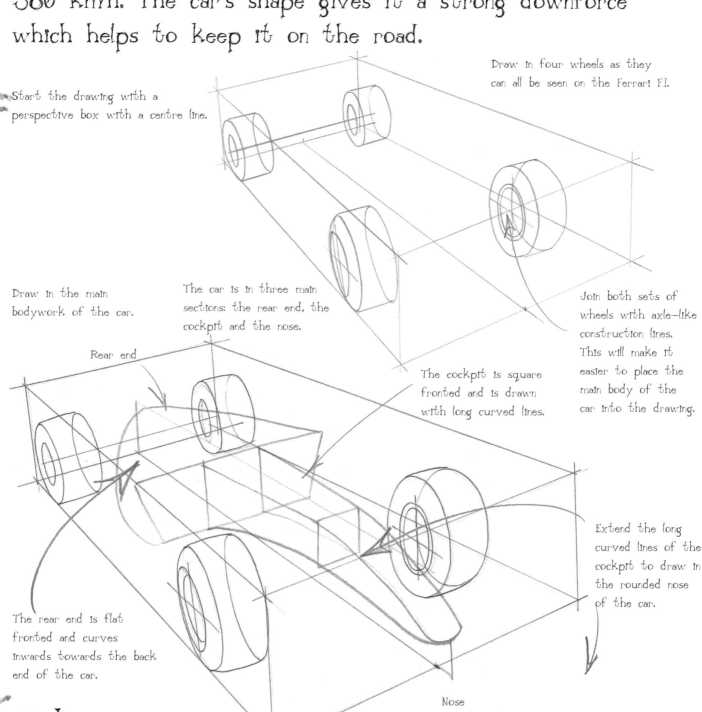

Michael Schumacher has won many races in Formula 1 driving the Ferrari F1. It can reach speeds of 360 km/h. The car's shape gives it a strong downforce which helps to keep it on the road.

Start the drawing with a perspective box with a centre line.

Draw in four wheels as they can all be seen on the Ferrari F1.

Draw in the main bodywork of the car.

The car is in three main sections: the rear end, the cockpit and the nose.

The cockpit is square fronted and is drawn with long curved lines.

Join both sets of wheels with axle-like construction lines. This will make it easier to place the main body of the car into the drawing.

Rear end

Extend the long curved lines of the cockpit to draw in the rounded nose of the car.

The rear end is flat fronted and curves inwards towards the back end of the car.

Nose

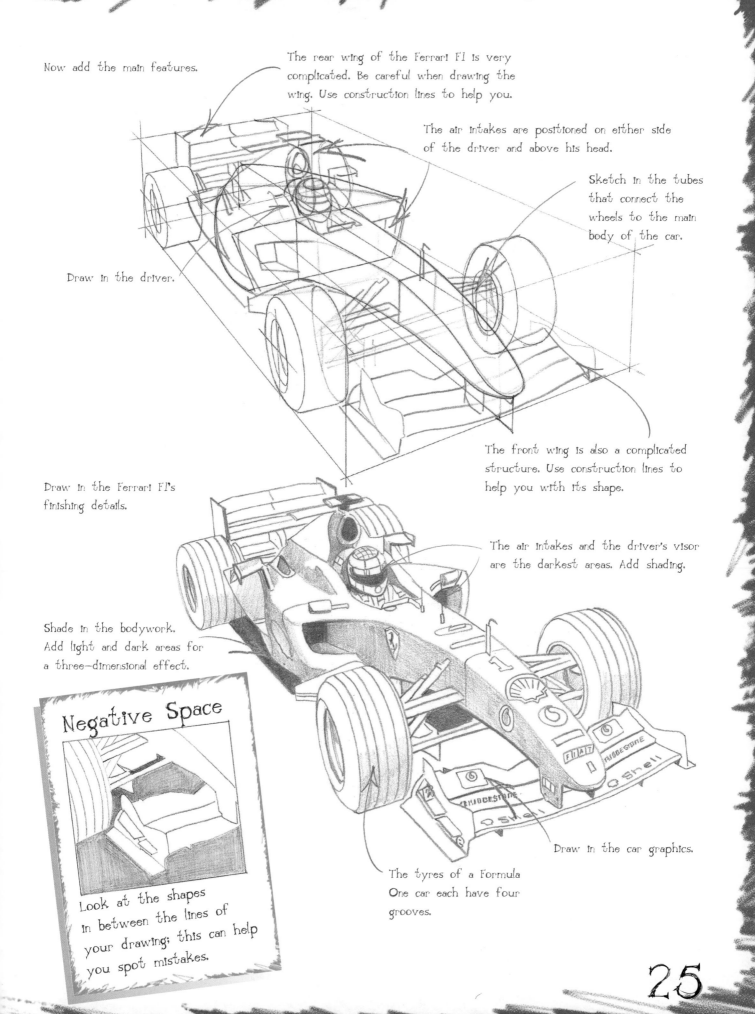

Now add the main features.

The rear wing of the Ferrari F1 is very complicated. Be careful when drawing the wing. Use construction lines to help you.

The air intakes are positioned on either side of the driver and above his head.

Sketch in the tubes that connect the wheels to the main body of the car.

Draw in the driver.

The front wing is also a complicated structure. Use construction lines to help you with its shape.

Draw in the Ferrari F1's finishing details.

The air intakes and the driver's visor are the darkest areas. Add shading.

Shade in the bodywork. Add light and dark areas for a three-dimensional effect.

Negative Space

Look at the shapes in between the lines of your drawing; this can help you spot mistakes.

Draw in the car graphics.

The tyres of a Formula One car each have four grooves.

Thrust DRAW SSC

The Thrust SSC set the new land speed record on 15 October 1997 at Black Rock Desert, Nevada. Its 100,000 bhp jet engines propelled the driver, Andy Green, to more than 997 km/h to make it the world's first supersonic land speed record.

First draw a long perspective box.

Start to draw in the jet engines on each side.

For each engine draw two ellipses, the rear one smaller than the front one. Then connect them with straight lines.

Mark in the centre line.

Add a triangle at the rear to form the car's fin.

Draw in the front part of each engine. Draw two smaller ellipses, one inside the other, and join them to the body of the engine with curved lines.

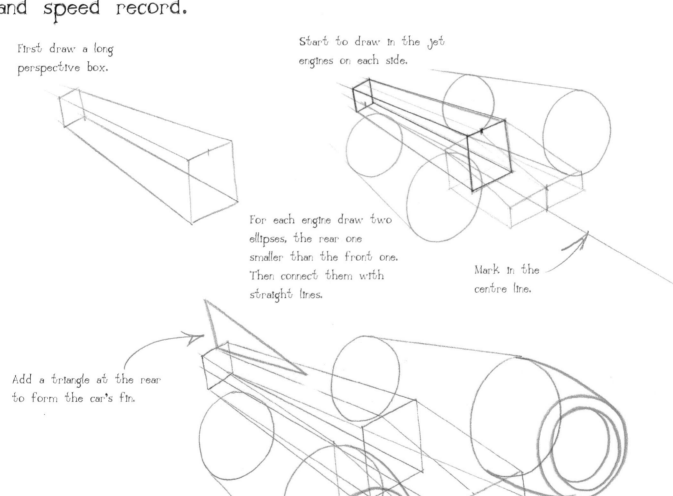

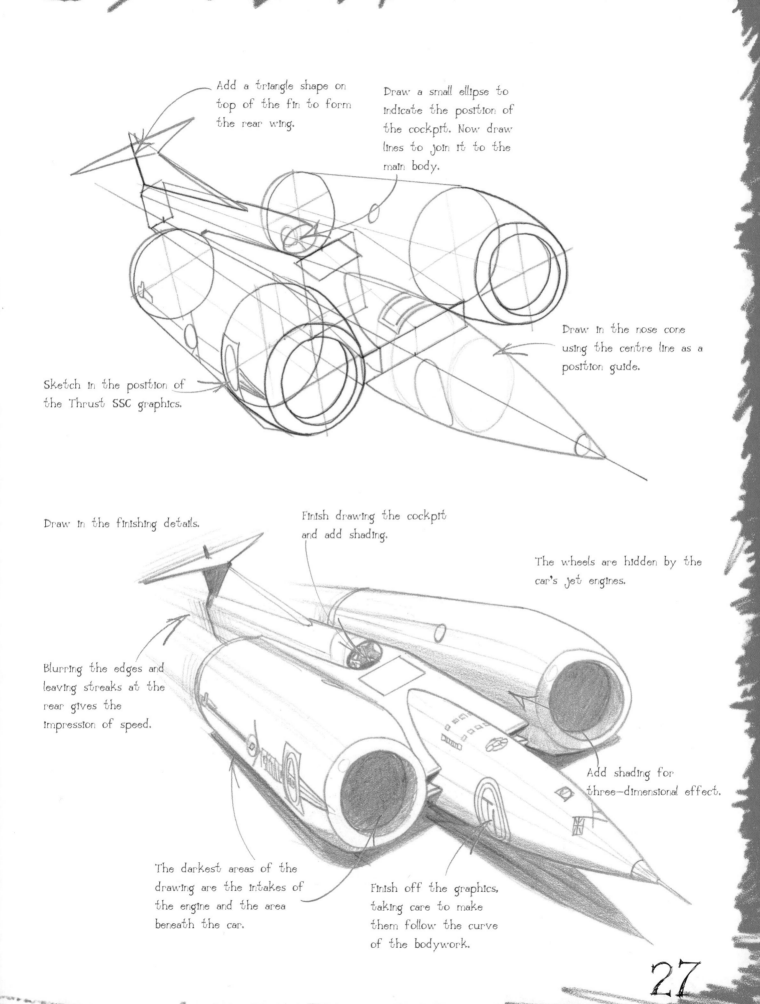

Add a triangle shape on top of the fin to form the rear wing.

Draw a small ellipse to indicate the position of the cockpit. Now draw lines to join it to the main body.

Draw in the nose cone using the centre line as a position guide.

Sketch in the position of the Thrust SSC graphics.

Draw in the finishing details.

Finish drawing the cockpit and add shading.

The wheels are hidden by the car's jet engines.

Blurring the edges and leaving streaks at the rear gives the impression of speed.

Add shading for three-dimensional effect.

The darkest areas of the drawing are the intakes of the engine and the area beneath the car.

Finish off the graphics, taking care to make them follow the curve of the bodywork.

Fokker DR1 Triplane

The Fokker Dreidecker (DR1) triplane was used by Germany in WW1 against the British Sopwith triplane. It carried one pilot and was armed with two machine guns. Its most famous pilot was Baron Manfred von Richthofen.

Start by drawing a cross, then draw a circle.

Centre line

Centre line

Nose

Centre line

Take a line from the centre of the cross, this is the centre line of the plane.

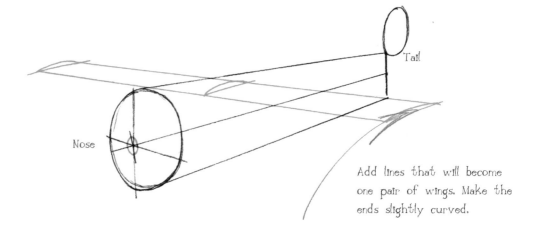

Tail

Nose

Add lines that will become one pair of wings. Make the ends slightly curved.

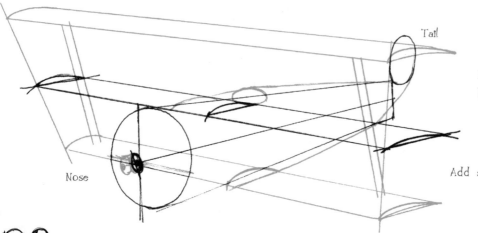

Tail

Nose

Now add lines that will become the other wings.

Add supports for the wings.

The DR1 was a difficult aircraft to fly, and was regarded as a machine strictly for experienced pilots.

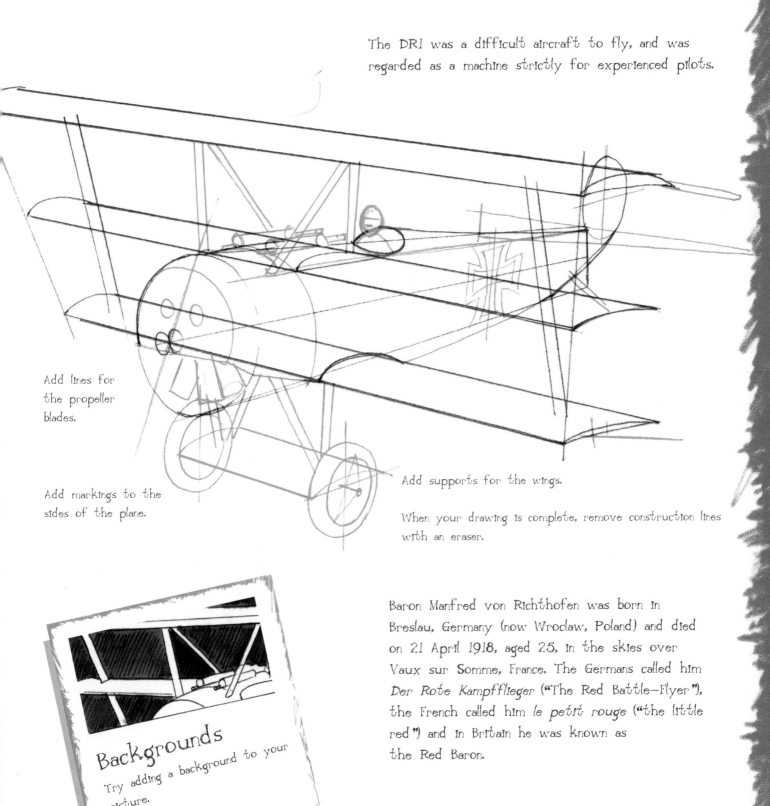

Add lines for the propeller blades.

Add markings to the sides of the plane.

Add supports for the wings.

When your drawing is complete, remove construction lines with an eraser.

Backgrounds
Try adding a background to your picture.

Baron Manfred von Richthofen was born in Breslau, Germany (now Wroclaw, Poland) and died on 21 April 1918, aged 25, in the skies over Vaux sur Somme, France. The Germans called him *Der Rote Kampfflieger* ("The Red Battle-Flyer"), the French called him *le petit rouge* ("the little red") and in Britain he was known as the Red Baron.

29

Supermarine *DRAW* Spitfire

In the summer of 1940, fewer than a thousand British Hurricanes and Supermarine Spitfire planes defeated 3,000 aircraft in the *Luftwaffe* (German airforce).

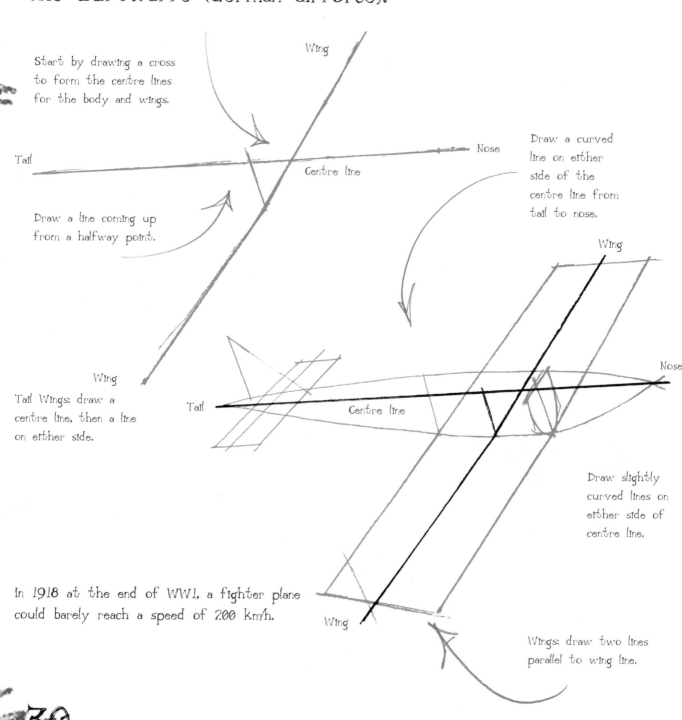

Start by drawing a cross to form the centre lines for the body and wings.

Wing

Tail

Centre line

Nose

Draw a curved line on either side of the centre line from tail to nose.

Draw a line coming up from a halfway point.

Wing

Tail Wings: draw a centre line, then a line on either side.

Wing

Tail

Centre line

Nose

Draw slightly curved lines on either side of centre line.

In 1918 at the end of WW1, a fighter plane could barely reach a speed of 200 km/h.

Wing

Wings: draw two lines parallel to wing line.

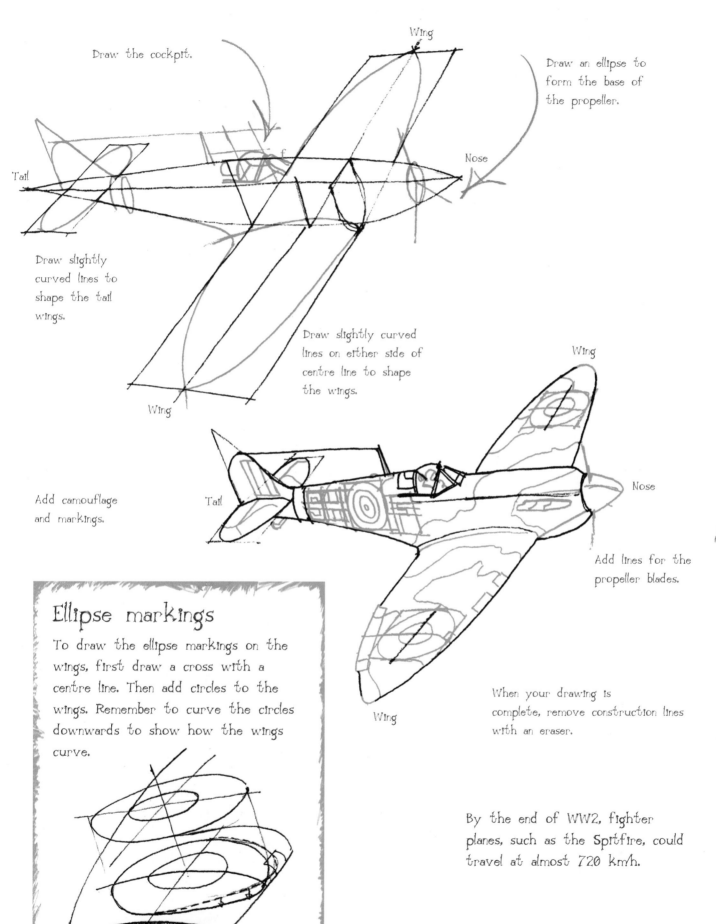

Draw the cockpit.

Wing

Draw an ellipse to form the base of the propeller.

Nose

Tail

Draw slightly curved lines to shape the tail wings.

Wing

Draw slightly curved lines on either side of centre line to shape the wings.

Wing

Add camouflage and markings.

Tail

Nose

Add lines for the propeller blades.

Ellipse markings

To draw the ellipse markings on the wings, first draw a cross with a centre line. Then add circles to the wings. Remember to curve the circles downwards to show how the wings curve.

Wing

When your drawing is complete, remove construction lines with an eraser.

By the end of WW2, fighter planes, such as the Spitfire, could travel at almost 720 km/h.

31

DRAW
Supermarine S6B

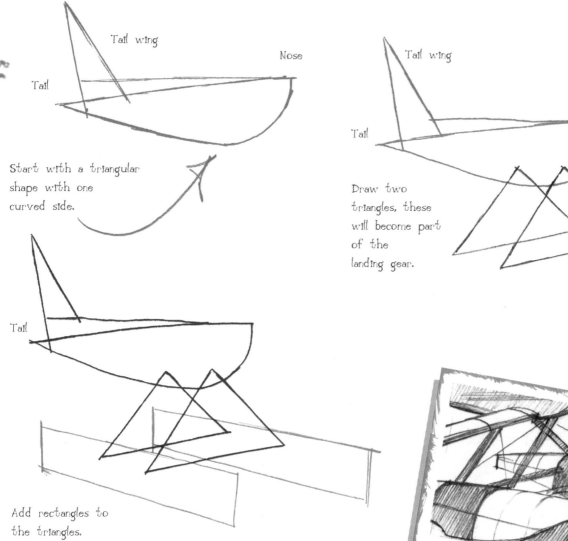

The Supermarine S6B Seaplane became the fastest aircraft on Earth in September 1931 when it achieved a record-breaking speed of 656 km/h.

Tail wing

Nose

Tail

Start with a triangular shape with one curved side.

Tail wing

Nose

Tail

Draw two triangles, these will become part of the landing gear.

Tail

Add rectangles to the triangles.

The Supermarine S6B won the Schneider Trophy Seaplane contests for speed over a set course, for the third successive year — and outright — on 12 September 1931.

Light and dark

Shading can make your drawing appear three-dimensional.

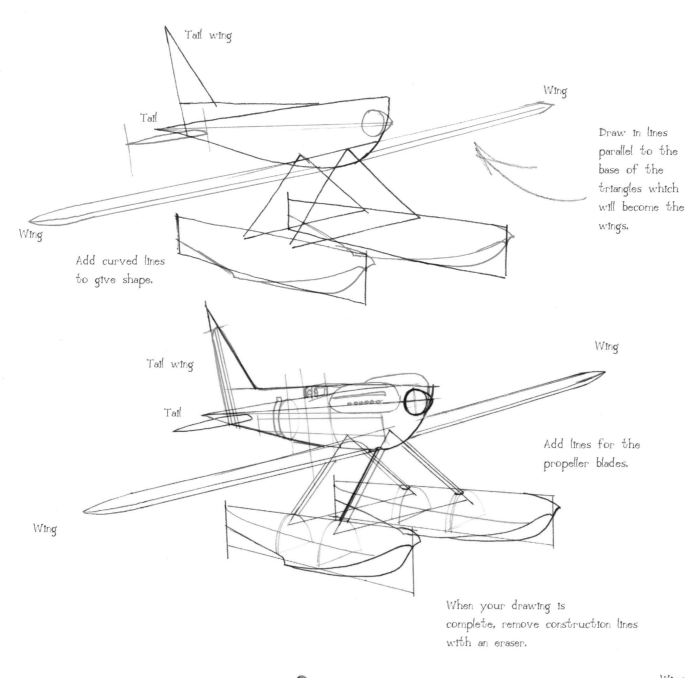

Tail wing

Tail

Wing

Wing

Draw in lines parallel to the base of the triangles which will become the wings.

Add curved lines to give shape.

Tail wing

Tail

Wing

Wing

Add lines for the propeller blades.

When your drawing is complete, remove construction lines with an eraser.

The S6B was designed by Reginald (R.J.) Mitchell. He later went on to design the Supermarine Spitfire fighter. The S6B had a Rolls-Royce R engine.

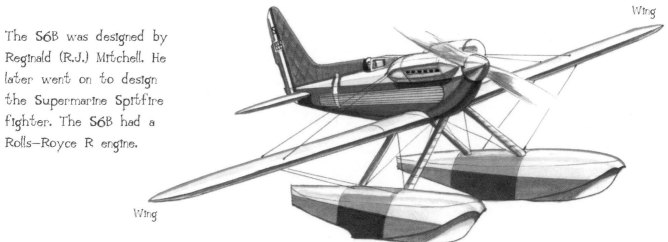

Wing

Wing

33

DRAW Pitts Special

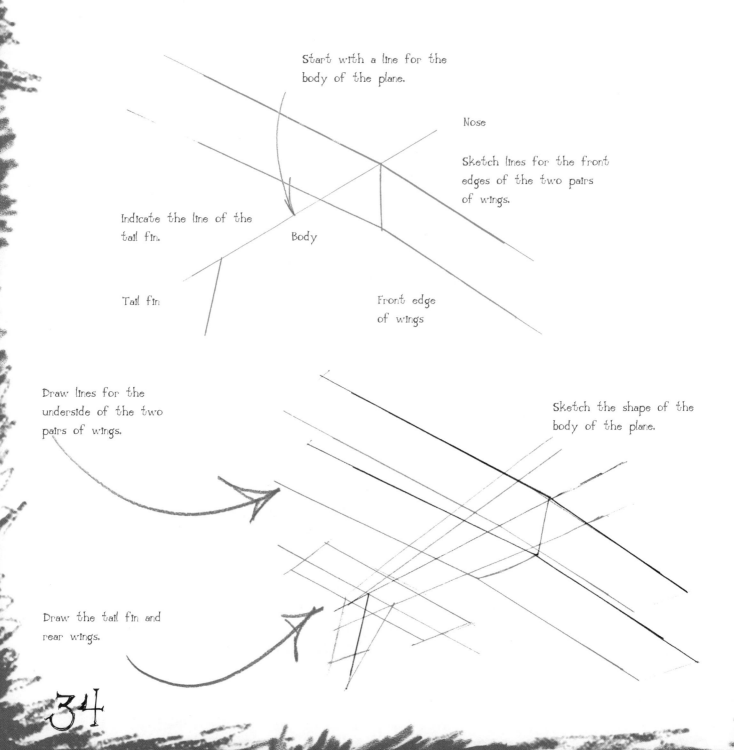

One of the world's most famous stunt planes, the Pitts Special, was designed in 1944 in Florida, by Curtis Pitts.

Start with a line for the body of the plane.

Nose

Sketch lines for the front edges of the two pairs of wings.

Indicate the line of the tail fin.

Body

Tail fin

Front edge of wings

Draw lines for the underside of the two pairs of wings.

Sketch the shape of the body of the plane.

Draw the tail fin and rear wings.

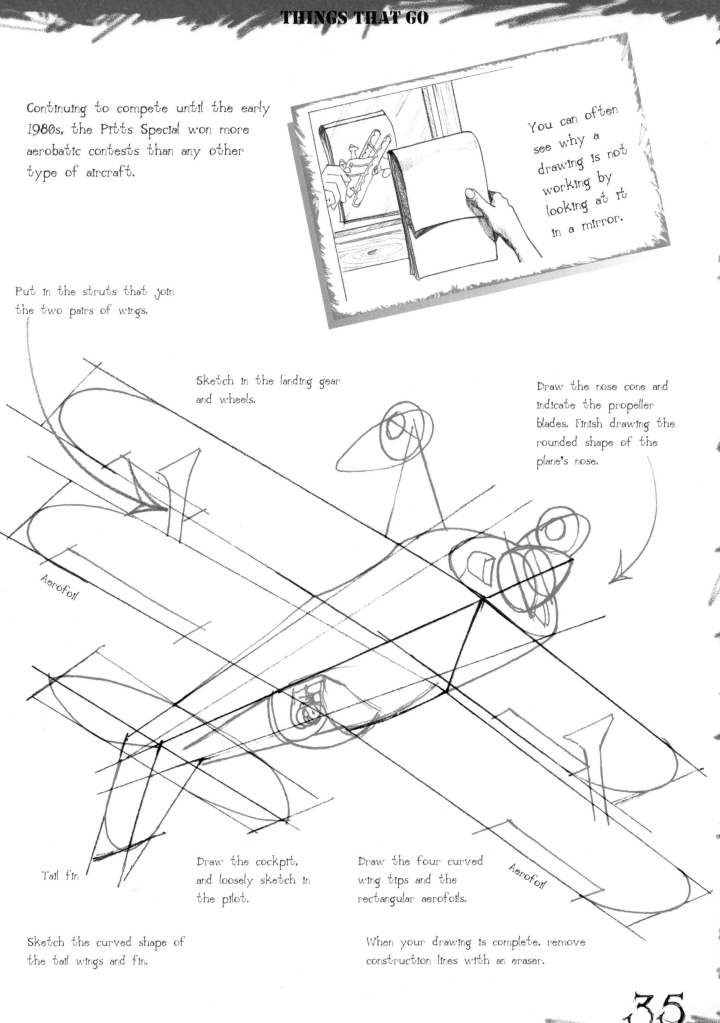

Continuing to compete until the early 1980s, the Pitts Special won more aerobatic contests than any other type of aircraft.

You can often see why a drawing is not working by looking at it in a mirror.

Put in the struts that join the two pairs of wings.

Sketch in the landing gear and wheels.

Draw the nose cone and indicate the propeller blades. Finish drawing the rounded shape of the plane's nose.

Aerofoil

Tail fin

Draw the cockpit, and loosely sketch in the pilot.

Draw the four curved wing tips and the rectangular aerofoils.

Aerofoil

Sketch the curved shape of the tail wings and fin.

When your drawing is complete, remove construction lines with an eraser.

DRAW
'Blackbird'

The Lockheed SR–71, or 'Blackbird', is the world's fastest jet plane. It reached a speed of 3,529 km/h, over three times the speed of sound, in 1976. The SR–71 was used for spying.

Draw a line for the rear of the plane's wing.

Tail

Draw a line on either side of the line of the body.

Body

Draw a longer line from the rear of the plane to its nose.

Nose

Draw two triangular shapes to indicate the tails on the engines.

Engine tail

Tail

Engine tail

Draw a large triangle to form the wings.

Draw two curved lines to make the front of the aircraft.

Sketch a rectangle from the nose of the plane to the rear. Make the shape slightly wider at the front.

Nose

36

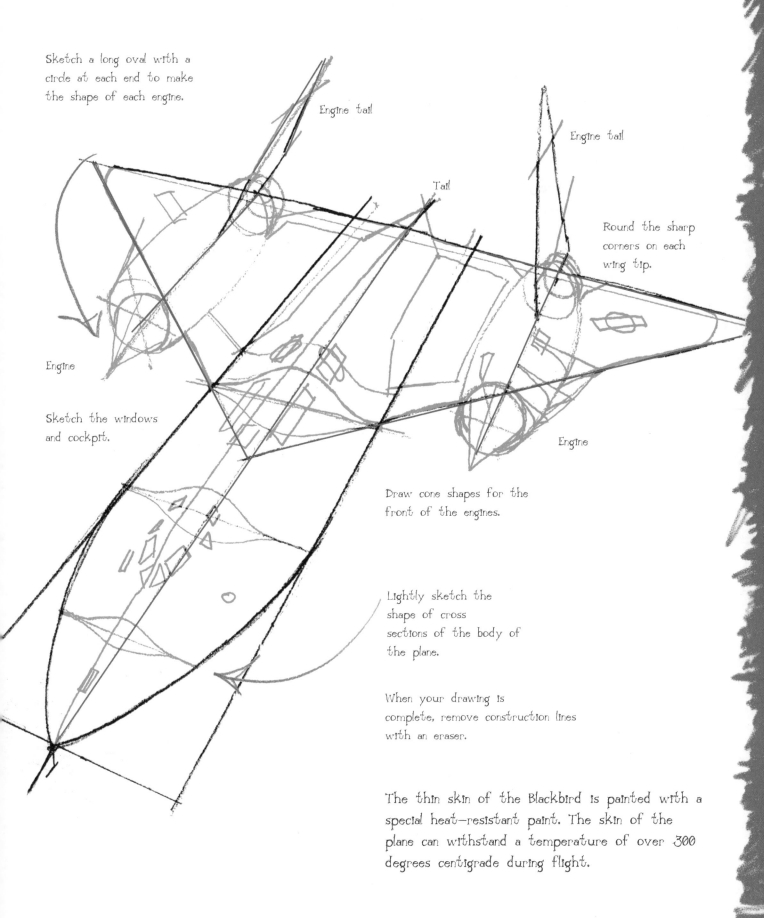

Sketch a long oval with a circle at each end to make the shape of each engine.

Engine tail

Engine tail

Tail

Round the sharp corners on each wing tip.

Engine

Sketch the windows and cockpit.

Engine

Draw cone shapes for the front of the engines.

Lightly sketch the shape of cross sections of the body of the plane.

When your drawing is complete, remove construction lines with an eraser.

The thin skin of the Blackbird is painted with a special heat-resistant paint. The skin of the plane can withstand a temperature of over 300 degrees centigrade during flight.

Concorde

DRAW

oncorde had four specially designed Rolls—Royce engines. These provided the extra power needed for take off and the transition to supersonic flight. It was the most powerful pure jet—engine flying commercially.

Draw a line from the nose of the Concorde to its rear.

Rear

Wings

Lightly sketch a large triangle to form the wings.

Nose

Draw the position of the tail fin.

Sketch in the body and the long pointed nose of Concorde.

Nose

Make a cardboard frame and use it on your drawing to find the best composition.

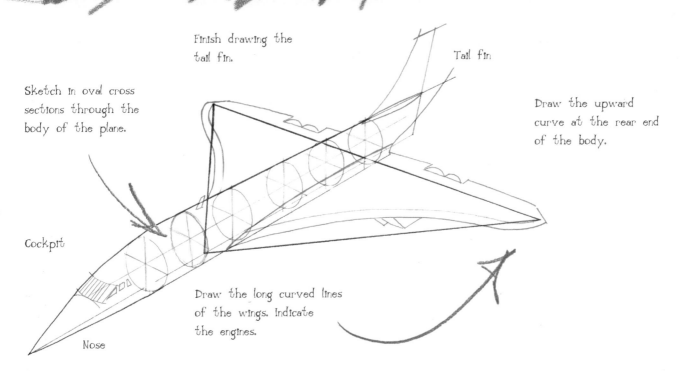

Finish drawing the
tail fin.

Tail fin

Sketch in oval cross
sections through the
body of the plane.

Draw the upward
curve at the rear end
of the body.

Cockpit

Draw the long curved lines
of the wings. Indicate
the engines.

Nose

Draw the windows in the cockpit.

When your drawing is
complete, remove construction lines
with an eraser.

The average flight time between London Heathrow and
New York JFK was three hours and 20 minutes.
Typically a Boeing 747 takes more than seven hours for
the same journey!

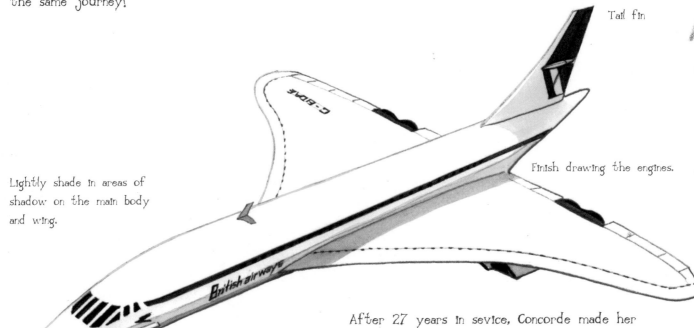

Tail fin

Lightly shade in areas of
shadow on the main body
and wing.

Finish drawing the engines.

Nose

Lastly, draw the plane's
markings.

After 27 years in sevice, Concorde made her
last flight between London and New York on
24 October 2003.

F—16A Fighting Falcon

DRAW

The F—16A Fighting Falcon is a compact and manoeuvrable fighter aircraft. It is highly effective in both air—to-air combat and air-to-surface attacks.

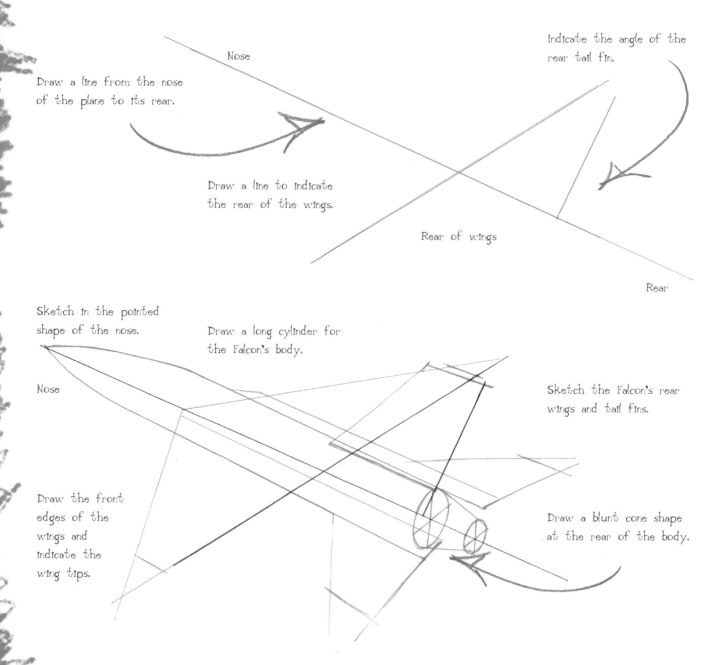

Draw a line from the nose of the plane to its rear.

Nose

Indicate the angle of the rear tail fin.

Draw a line to indicate the rear of the wings.

Rear of wings

Rear

Sketch in the pointed shape of the nose.

Draw a long cylinder for the Falcon's body.

Nose

Sketch the Falcon's rear wings and tail fins.

Draw the front edges of the wings and indicate the wing tips.

Draw a blunt cone shape at the rear of the body.

40

Side View

Do quick sketches of the plane from different viewpoints so you can become familiar with its basic shape.

The F-16A can accurately locate targets in all weathers and detect hard-to-find, low flying aircraft. It can also fly more than 860 km without needing to stop and refuel.

Draw the cockpit and put in the pilot.

Lightly sketch the cross section of the body of the plane.

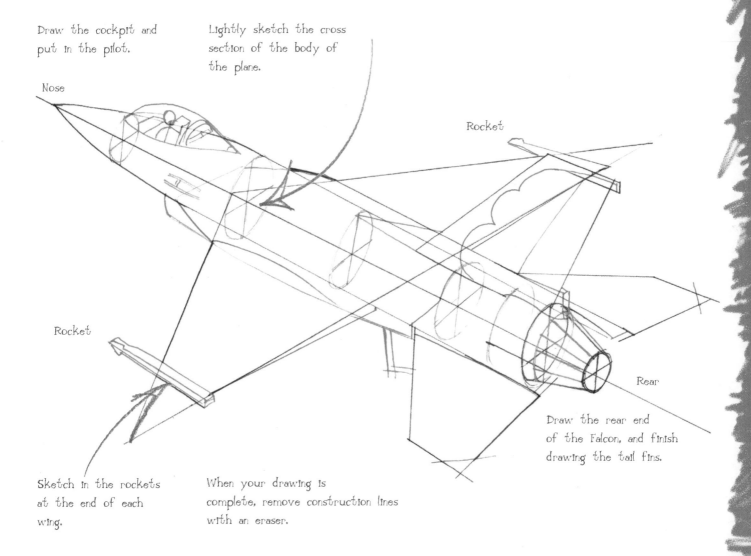

Nose

Rocket

Rocket

Rear

Draw the rear end of the Falcon, and finish drawing the tail fins.

Sketch in the rockets at the end of each wing.

When your drawing is complete, remove construction lines with an eraser.

Airbus A380
DRAW

The 555 seat, double-decker Airbus A380 will be the world's largest passenger carrying airliner.

Draw the back pair of wings.

Draw a line from the rear of the plane to its nose.

Tail

Nose

Draw the front pair of wings.

Several variations of A380 planes are planned, the basic aircraft is the 555 seat A380-800. It can fly 15,000 km without refuelling.

Indicate the angle of the rear tail fin.

Tail

Ellipse

Ellipse

Ellipse

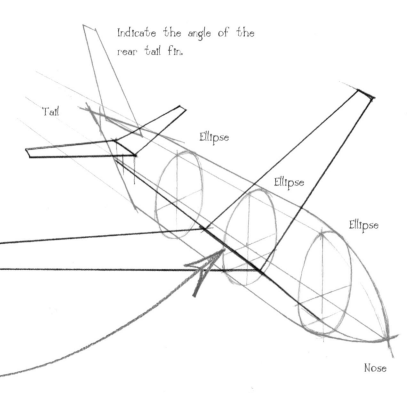

Draw in three ellipses, then join them together to form the body of the plane.

Nose

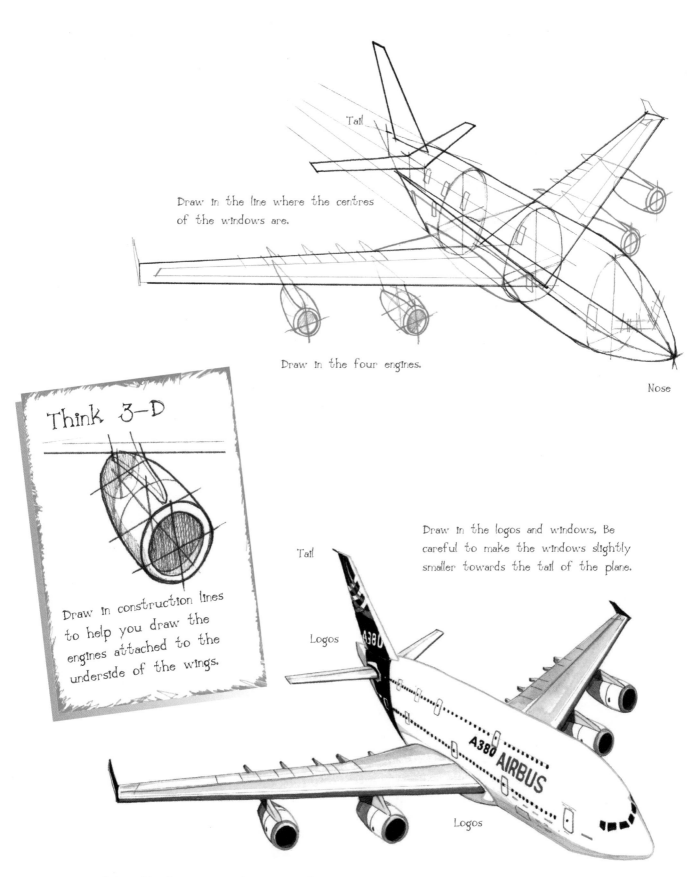

Tail

Draw in the line where the centres of the windows are.

Draw in the four engines.

Nose

Think 3–D

Draw in construction lines to help you draw the engines attached to the underside of the wings.

Tail

Logos

Draw in the logos and windows, Be careful to make the windows slightly smaller towards the tail of the plane.

A380 AIRBUS

Logos

Nose

The A380 will be able to use existing airports, they have also been designed to create lower fuel emissions and less noise.

When your drawing is complete, remove construction lines with an eraser.

43

Space Ship One
DRAW

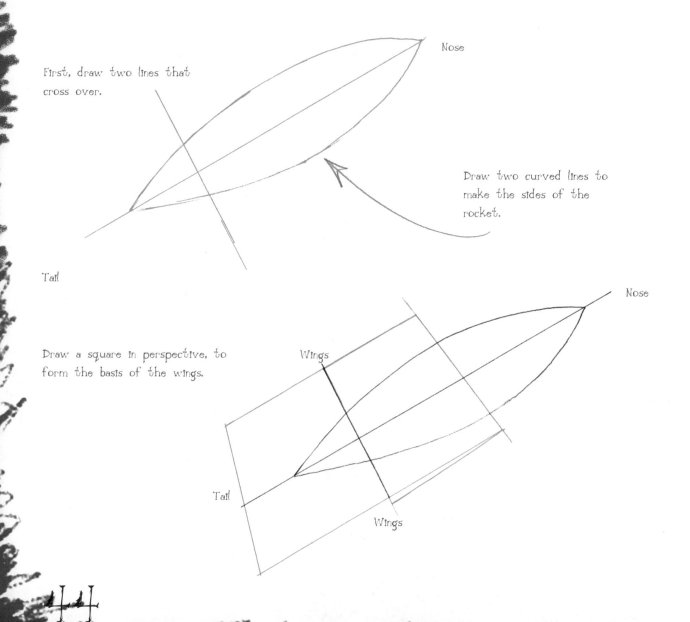

Space Ship One made the first privately-funded space flight on 21 June 2004. It is hoped that this is the future of space tourism. Thousands of people are expected to leave the Earth's atmosphere each year.

First, draw two lines that cross over.

Nose

Draw two curved lines to make the sides of the rocket.

Tail

Draw a square in perspective, to form the basis of the wings.

Wings

Nose

Tail

Wings

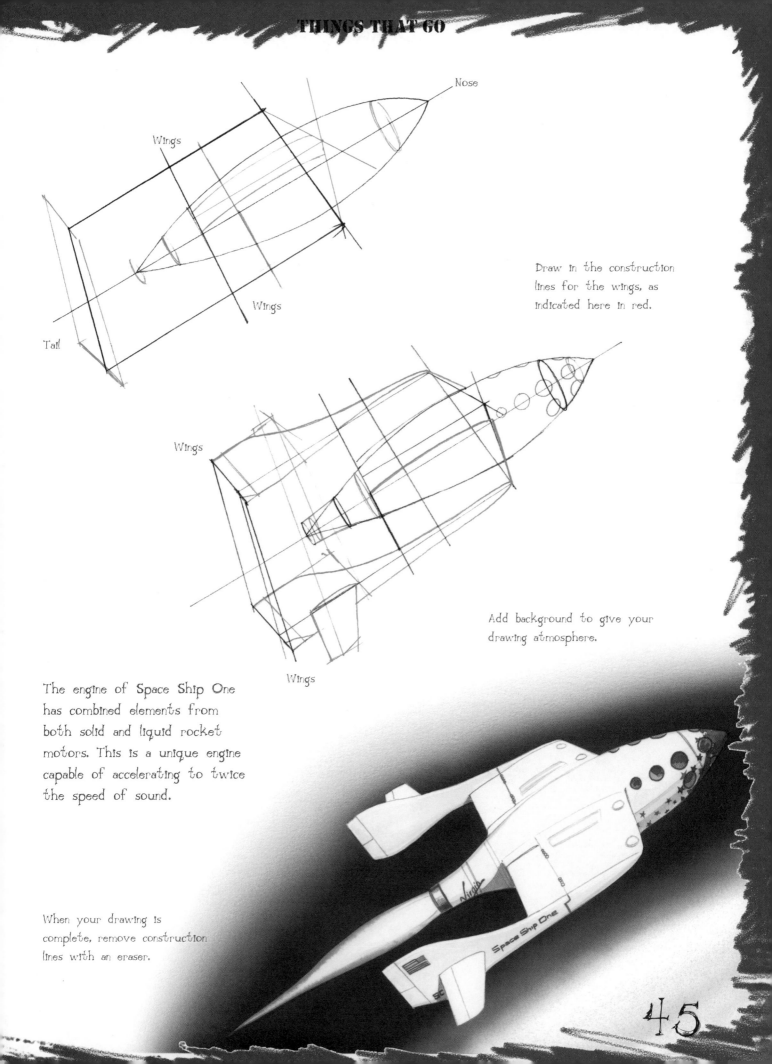

Nose

Wings

Wings

Tail

Draw in the construction lines for the wings, as indicated here in red.

Wings

Wings

Add background to give your drawing atmosphere.

The engine of Space Ship One has combined elements from both solid and liquid rocket motors. This is a unique engine capable of accelerating to twice the speed of sound.

When your drawing is complete, remove construction lines with an eraser.

45

DRAW Speedboat

Speedboats are designed to move quickly through the water. They are propelled by powerful motors at the stern.

First draw a three-dimensional rectangular box. Then draw a line through the centre.

Using the centre line as a starting point, draw long curved lines to show the shape of the boat.

The stern (rear) of the boat is drawn in with straight lines.

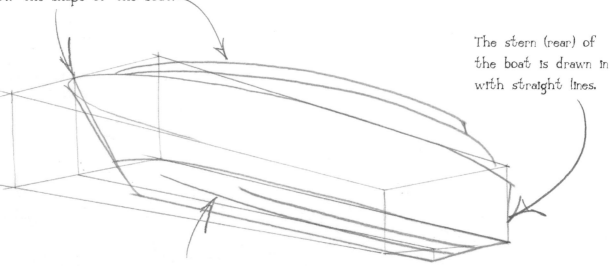

Draw straight lines on the bottom of the rectangular box to mark the bottom of the boat.

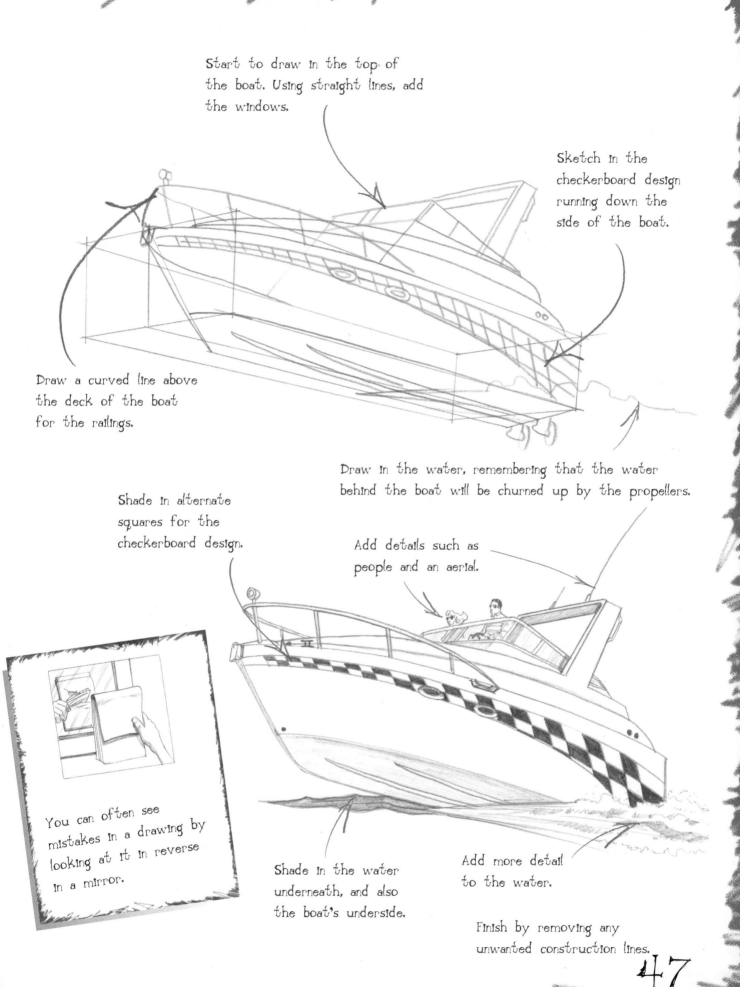

Start to draw in the top of the boat. Using straight lines, add the windows.

Sketch in the checkerboard design running down the side of the boat.

Draw a curved line above the deck of the boat for the railings.

Draw in the water, remembering that the water behind the boat will be churned up by the propellers.

Shade in alternate squares for the checkerboard design.

Add details such as people and an aerial.

You can often see mistakes in a drawing by looking at it in reverse in a mirror.

Shade in the water underneath, and also the boat's underside.

Add more detail to the water.

Finish by removing any unwanted construction lines.

47

DRAW Racing yacht

Yacht races are held all around the world. The yachts used are specially designed to take full advantage of the wind and move very fast through the water.

Mast

Draw two long lines for the mast.

Start by drawing a narrow rectangle for the hull.

Draw in a straight line for the water.

Add a line to form a small triangle to make the stern of the boat.

Draw a straight line down from the mast to the bow (front) of the boat.

Add a straight line coming down from the top of the mast to the stern of the boat.

Add curves to the bow of the boat.

Add the keel.

Add a small rudder.

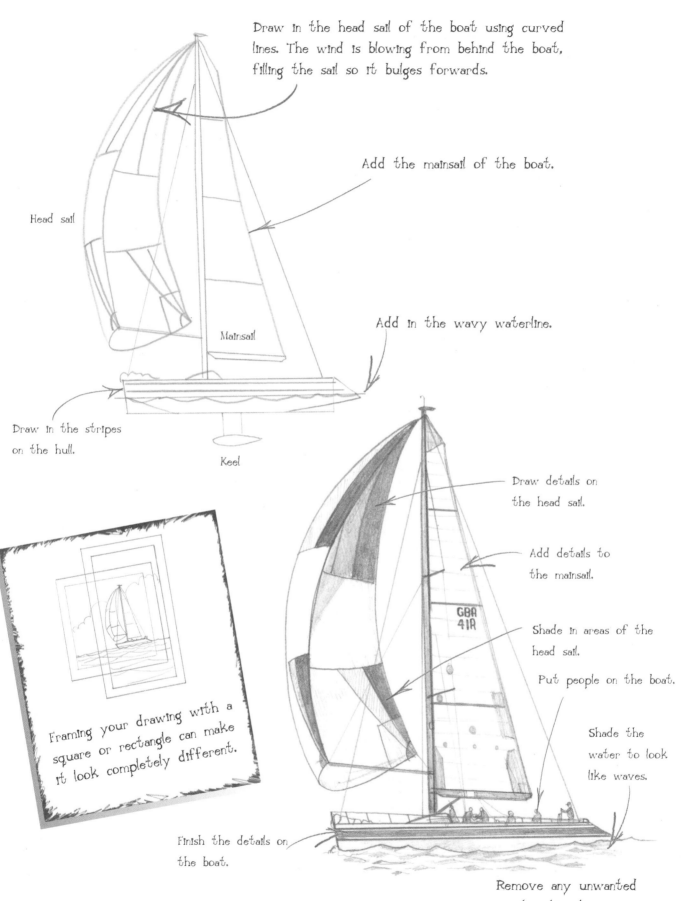

Draw in the head sail of the boat using curved lines. The wind is blowing from behind the boat, filling the sail so it bulges forwards.

Add the mainsail of the boat.

Head sail

Add in the wavy waterline.

Mainsail

Draw in the stripes on the hull.

Keel

Draw details on the head sail.

Add details to the mainsail.

GBA 41R

Shade in areas of the head sail.

Put people on the boat.

Shade the water to look like waves.

Framing your drawing with a square or rectangle can make it look completely different.

Finish the details on the boat.

Remove any unwanted construction lines.

49

DRAW Rowing boat

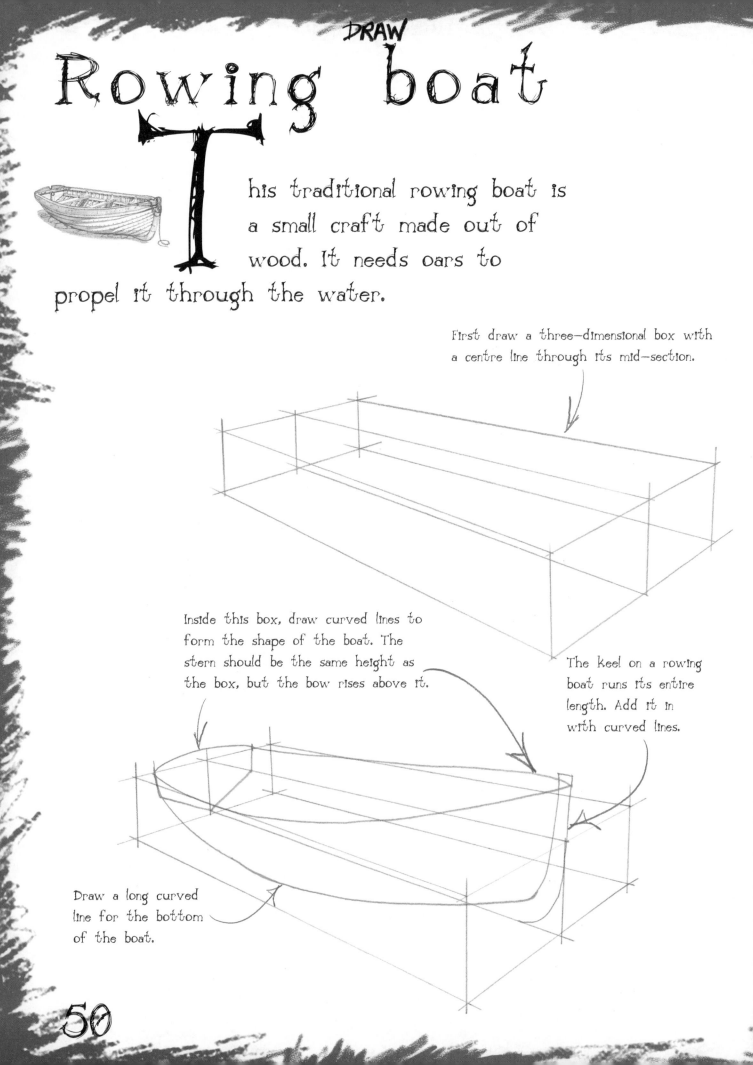

This traditional rowing boat is a small craft made out of wood. It needs oars to propel it through the water.

First draw a three-dimensional box with a centre line through its mid-section.

Inside this box, draw curved lines to form the shape of the boat. The stern should be the same height as the box, but the bow rises above it.

The keel on a rowing boat runs its entire length. Add it in with curved lines.

Draw a long curved line for the bottom of the boat.

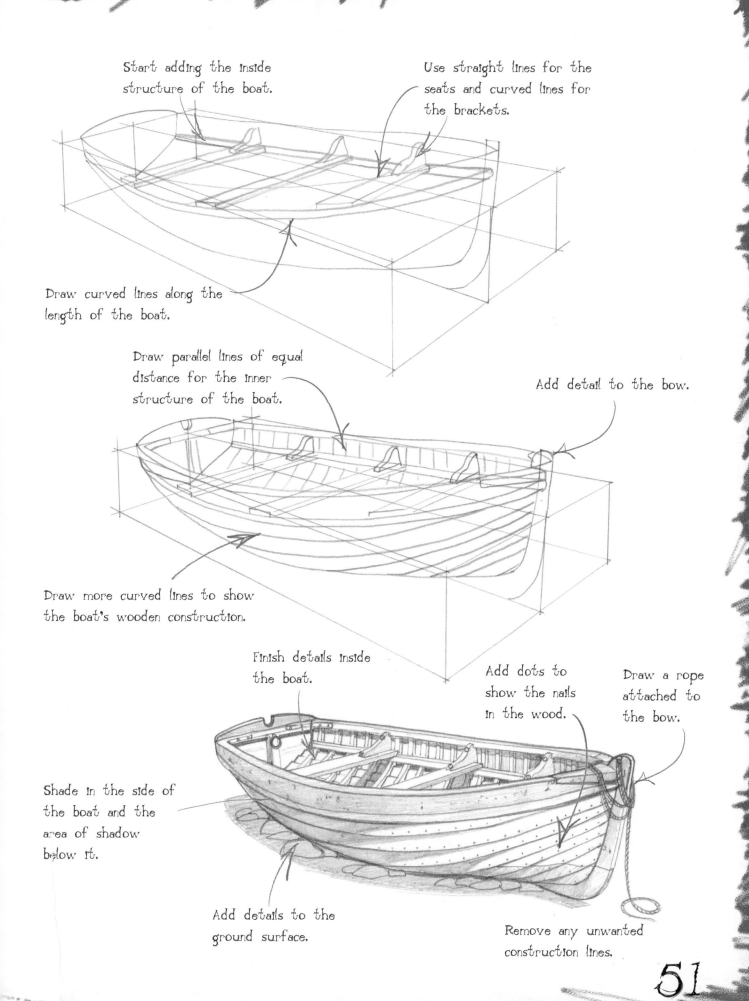

Start adding the inside structure of the boat.

Use straight lines for the seats and curved lines for the brackets.

Draw curved lines along the length of the boat.

Draw parallel lines of equal distance for the inner structure of the boat.

Add detail to the bow.

Draw more curved lines to show the boat's wooden construction.

Finish details inside the boat.

Add dots to show the nails in the wood.

Draw a rope attached to the bow.

Shade in the side of the boat and the area of shadow below it.

Add details to the ground surface.

Remove any unwanted construction lines.

Topsail schooner

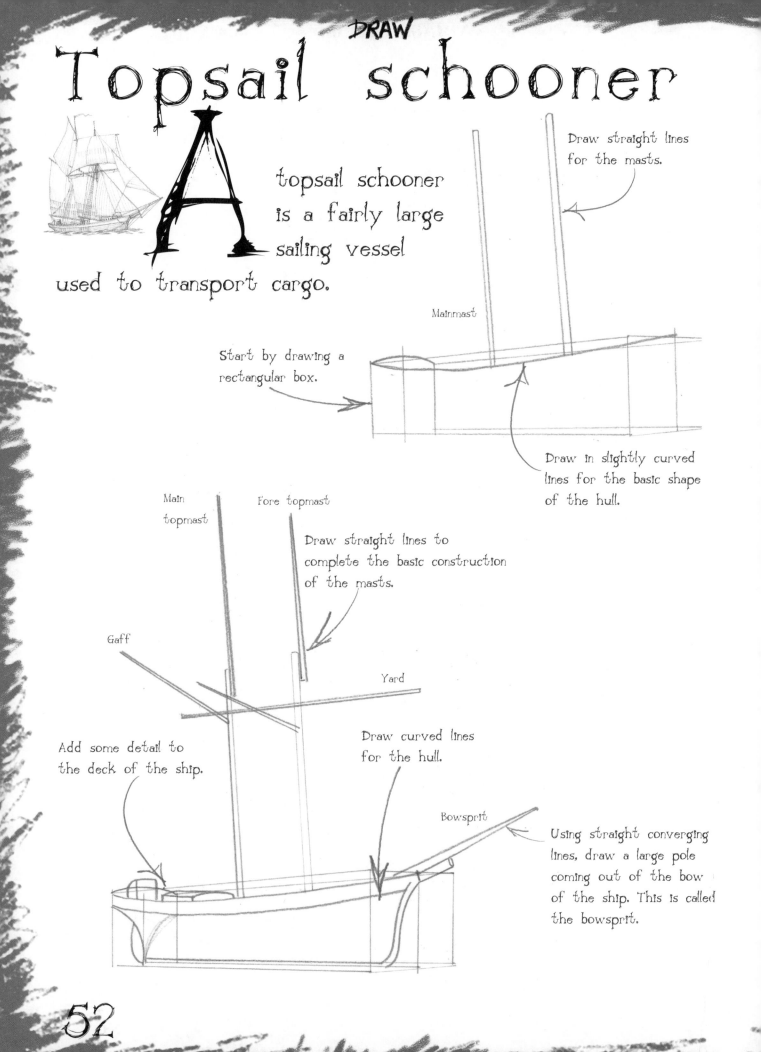

DRAW

A topsail schooner is a fairly large sailing vessel used to transport cargo.

Draw straight lines for the masts.

Mainmast

Start by drawing a rectangular box.

Draw in slightly curved lines for the basic shape of the hull.

Main topmast

Fore topmast

Draw straight lines to complete the basic construction of the masts.

Gaff

Yard

Add some detail to the deck of the ship.

Draw curved lines for the hull.

Bowsprit

Using straight converging lines, draw a large pole coming out of the bow of the ship. This is called the bowsprit.

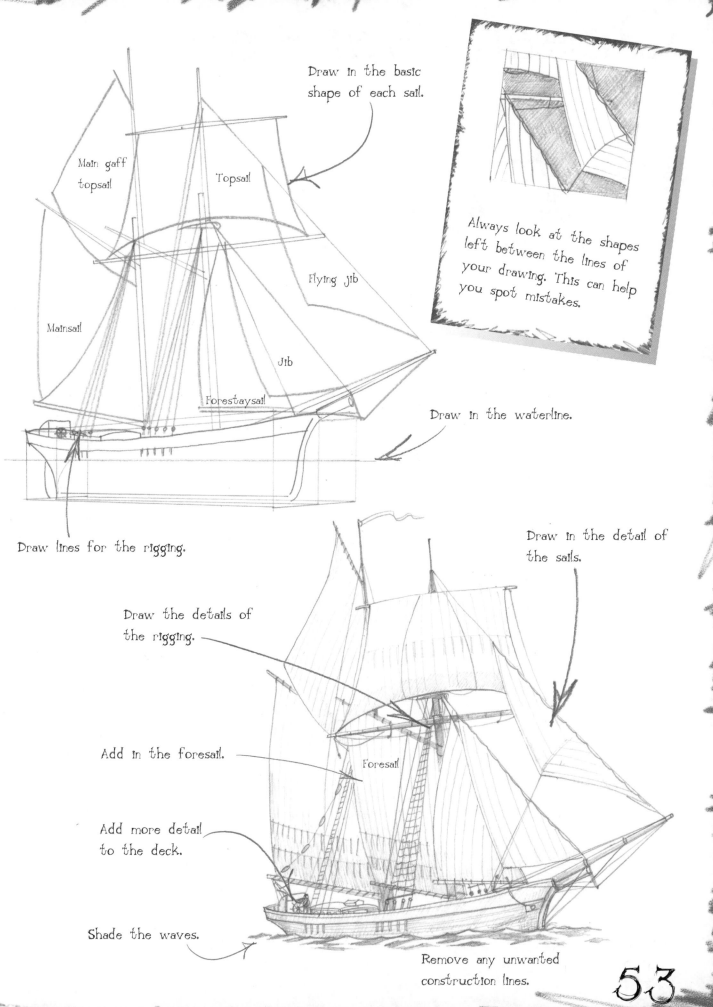

Draw in the basic shape of each sail.

Main gaff topsail

Topsail

Always look at the shapes left between the lines of your drawing. This can help you spot mistakes.

Flying jib

Mainsail

Jib

Forestaysail

Draw in the waterline.

Draw lines for the rigging.

Draw in the detail of the sails.

Draw the details of the rigging.

Add in the foresail.

Foresail

Add more detail to the deck.

Shade the waves.

Remove any unwanted construction lines.

53

Ocean tanker
DRAW

An ocean tanker is a massive ship used to transport huge amounts of fuel.

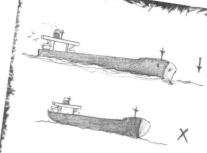

Ships and water
To make your drawing look authentic: the ship should always be sitting in the water, not on top of it.

Start your drawing with a large rectangular box with a centre line through the mid-section.

Draw a curved lip to indicate the top of the bow.

Using the lines of your original rectangular box as a guide, draw box shapes on the ship's deck where the superstructure will be.

Draw curved lines to mark the shape of the ship's bow.

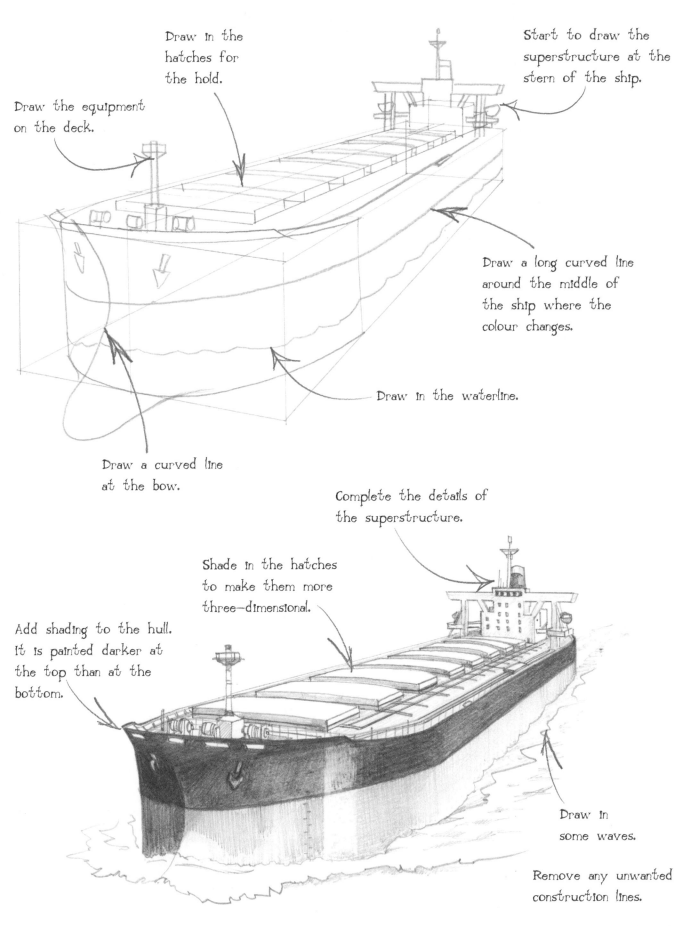

Draw in the hatches for the hold.

Start to draw the superstructure at the stern of the ship.

Draw the equipment on the deck.

Draw a long curved line around the middle of the ship where the colour changes.

Draw in the waterline.

Draw a curved line at the bow.

Complete the details of the superstructure.

Shade in the hatches to make them more three-dimensional.

Add shading to the hull. It is painted darker at the top than at the bottom.

Draw in some waves.

Remove any unwanted construction lines.

Fishing boat
DRAW

This small fishing boat is a working vessel that travels out to sea to try to catch a good haul of fish.

Start your drawing with a three-dimensional rectangular box with a centre line through the mid-section.

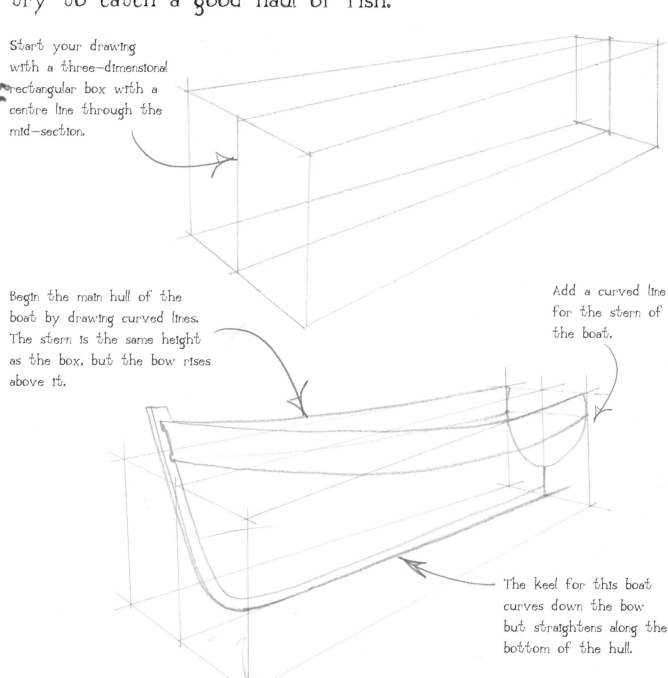

Begin the main hull of the boat by drawing curved lines. The stern is the same height as the box, but the bow rises above it.

Add a curved line for the stern of the boat.

The keel for this boat curves down the bow but straightens along the bottom of the hull.

Add a small house-like structure at the bow.

Add the main bridge structure to the deck.

Add more curved lines to the side of the boat.

Draw straight lines for the ropes of the fishing equipment.

Use straight lines to draw in the arms of the fishing equipment.

Draw in the winch machinery.

Add detail to the bridge.

Darken the underside of the lines on the side of the boat to give a realistic shadow effect.

Add in the water surface.

Remove any unwanted construction lines.

57

Draw Ocean liner

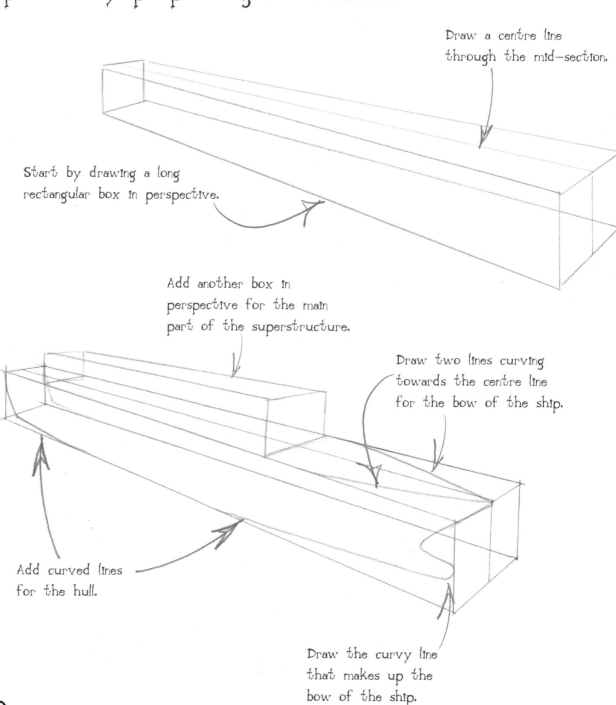

This luxury ocean liner is a large sea-going vessel designed to transport many people in great comfort.

Draw a centre line through the mid-section.

Start by drawing a long rectangular box in perspective.

Add another box in perspective for the main part of the superstructure.

Draw two lines curving towards the centre line for the bow of the ship.

Add curved lines for the hull.

Draw the curvy line that makes up the bow of the ship.

Add the funnels.

Add detail to the front of the main superstructure.

Draw in the waterline.

Add guidelines along the upper decks to help you position the windows.

Sketch in a line for the window of the bridge.

Add in small shapes for the lifeboats.

Using the straight lines as a guide, finish the detail of the windows.

Complete the details of the superstructure.

Add tone to the drawing to give it more impact.

Add in small dots for the portholes.

Add small areas of shading to represent the waves.

Remove any unwanted construction lines.

59

Pirate ship

Pirate ships were generally small, fast ships like sloops that were easy to manoeuvre. Large merchant ships tended to be heavier and slower so they were easy targets for pirates to attack.

Add three lines for the masts.

Draw a long box-like shape on two levels for the ship's hull.

See pages 8–9 to put perspective into use.

Using a high vanishing point, draw in the sails.

Draw in the bowsprit.

Draw in the different deck levels.

Start sketching in the ship's details now.

By framing your drawing with a square or a rectangle you can make it look completely different.

Draw a centre line through the sails.

Draw in straight lines for the rigging.

Add a flag at the rear.

Add lines along the shape of the hull to define it.

Finish off the detail on the rigging and add masts and rails.

Add detail to the sails.

Draw a skull and crossbones on the flag.

Draw in the decking.

Add cannon ports.

61

Fire engine

A fire engine is designed to pump water mechanically, using a powerful engine. This American fire truck has an extendable ladder on a turntable.

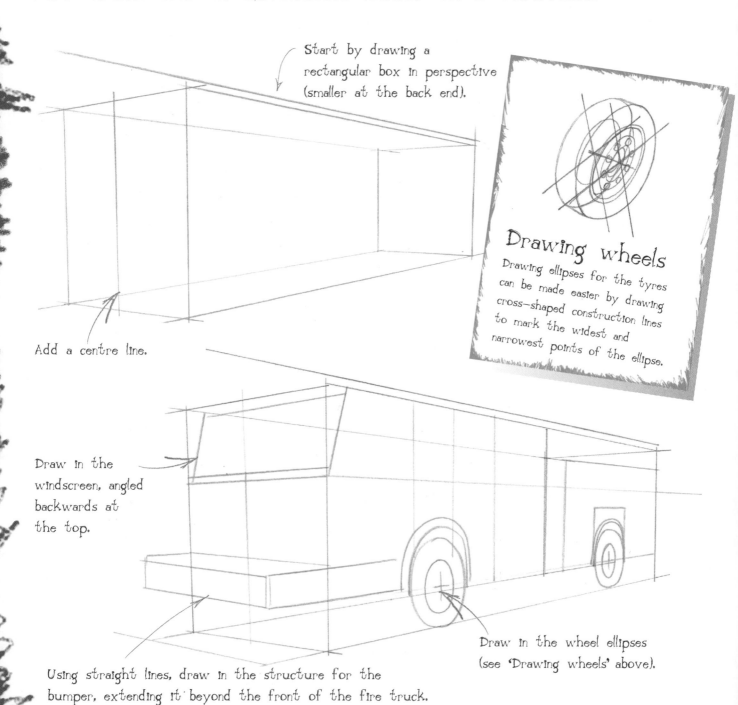

Start by drawing a rectangular box in perspective (smaller at the back end).

Add a centre line.

Drawing wheels

Drawing ellipses for the tyres can be made easier by drawing cross-shaped construction lines to mark the widest and narrowest points of the ellipse.

Draw in the windscreen, angled backwards at the top.

Draw in the wheel ellipses (see 'Drawing wheels' above).

Using straight lines, draw in the structure for the bumper, extending it beyond the front of the fire truck.

For the ladder, draw a long box in perspective on top of the fire truck. It extends beyond the front bumper and stops short of the rear of the truck. Draw in the details of the ladder.

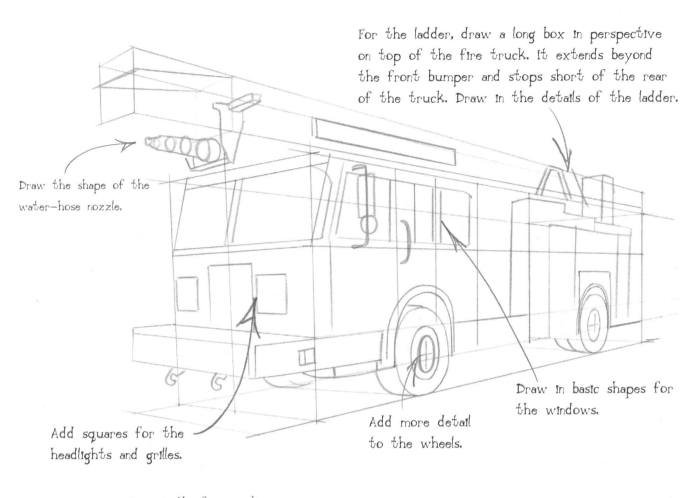

Draw the shape of the water-hose nozzle.

Draw in basic shapes for the windows.

Add more detail to the wheels.

Add squares for the headlights and grilles.

Draw in the framework of the ladder.

Add shading to windows, leaving a highlight on the glass where it is curved.

Finish drawing the windows and doors.

Draw in the controls for the firefighting equipment.

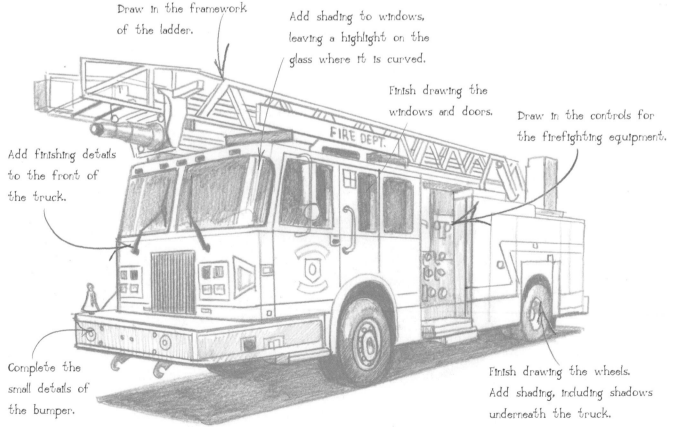

Add finishing details to the front of the truck.

Complete the small details of the bumper.

Finish drawing the wheels. Add shading, including shadows underneath the truck.

63

Articulated DRAW truck

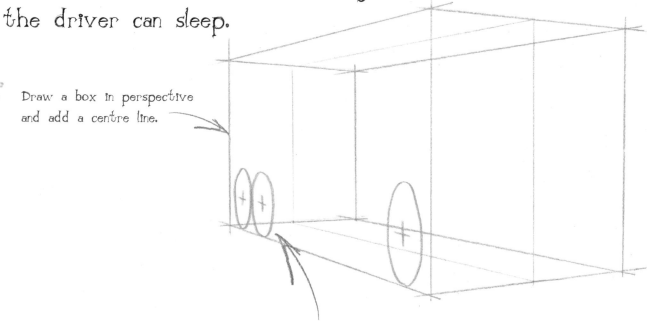

This typically American articulated truck is very powerful and can pull many different types of trailer. The truck also has a large cab in which the driver can sleep.

Draw a box in perspective and add a centre line.

Draw in the wheel ellipses.

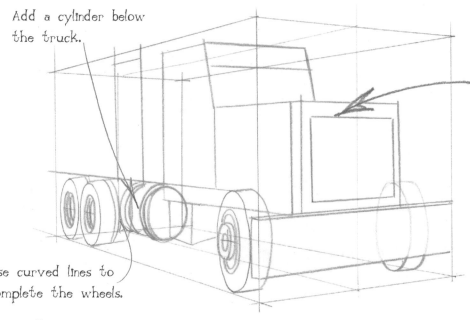

Add a cylinder below the truck.

Using your original box as a guide, start to draw in the recessed shape of the truck using straight lines.

Use curved lines to complete the wheels.

Add a large exhaust pipe on either side of the cab.

Draw in the windows.

Add circles for the headlights.

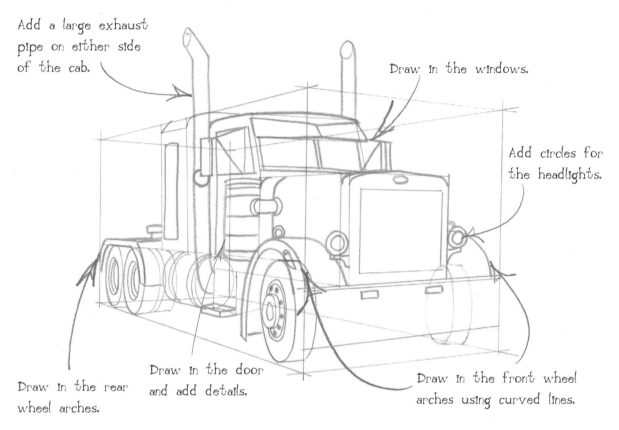

Draw in the rear wheel arches.

Draw in the door and add details.

Draw in the front wheel arches using curved lines.

Add shading to one side of the exhaust pipes.

Finish the detail on the windows.

Using straight lines and heavy shading, draw in the front grille.

Add the details to the cab.

Complete small details such as the headlights.

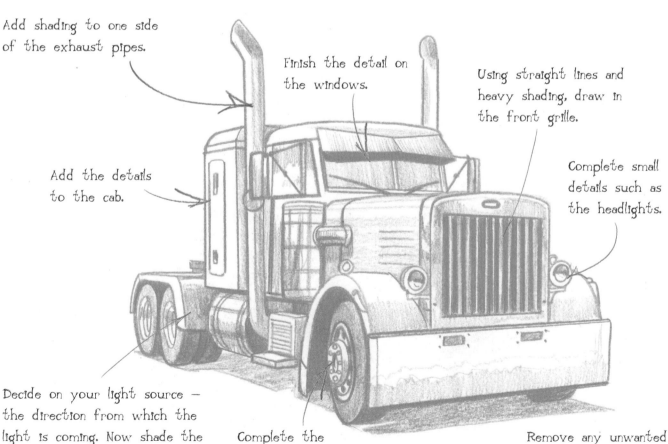

Decide on your light source — the direction from which the light is coming. Now shade the areas that face away from the light source.

Complete the wheel details.

Remove any unwanted construction lines.

DRAW Racing truck

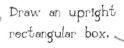

A racing truck can be tuned up to 1,300 brake horsepower. It uses four times as much diesel fuel as a standard truck.

Draw an upright rectangular box.

Draw a horizontal rectangular box, joining on to the first one.

Draw in the windscreen, using lines that curve gently.

Add in the side windows.

Draw in a double set of wheels at the rear.

Start to draw in the cab with simple shapes.

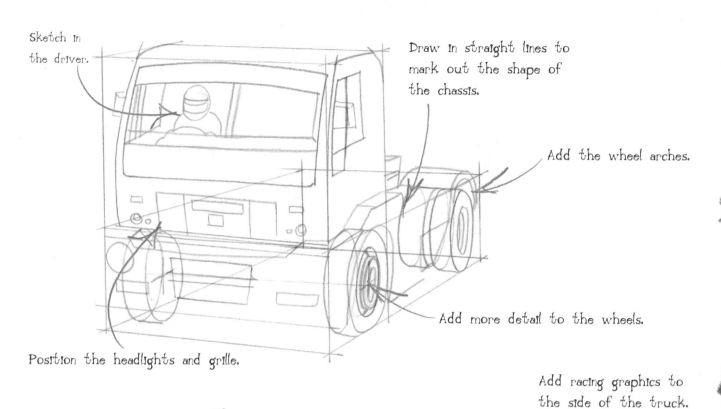

Sketch in the driver.

Draw in straight lines to mark out the shape of the chassis.

Add the wheel arches.

Add more detail to the wheels.

Position the headlights and grille.

Framing your drawing with a square or rectangle can make it look completely different.

Add racing graphics to the side of the truck.

Darken the inside of the cab, highlighting the driver.

Complete the details on the side of the truck.

Complete the details on the front of the truck, including graphics.

Add in the kerb of the racetrack.

Shade areas that face away from the light source.

Remove any unwanted construction lines.

67

DRAW
Snow plough

Snow ploughs are converted trucks with a curved plough attached to the front that pushes the snow away.

Start by drawing a box in perspective.

Add a centre line.

Sketch the cab using simple shapes.

Add two straight lines for the bed of the truck.

You can often see mistakes in a drawing by looking at it in reverse in a mirror.

Add two straight lines for the positions of the windscreen and radiator grille.

Draw in two wheel ellipses at the rear and one at the front.

Draw in the metal container at the rear of the truck using your construction lines as a guide.

Sketch in the exhaust pipe.

Sketch in the wing mirrors.

Add basic details to the front: badge, grille, headlights, etc.

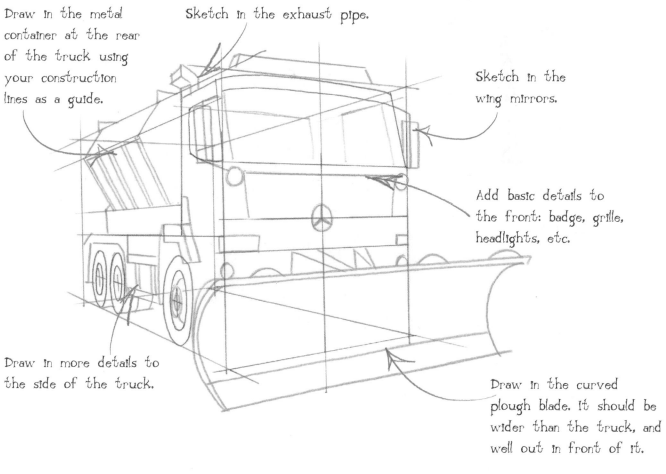

Draw in more details to the side of the truck.

Draw in the curved plough blade. It should be wider than the truck, and well out in front of it.

Add shading to the windows to show the shapes inside the cab.

Add shading to areas where the light source would not reach.

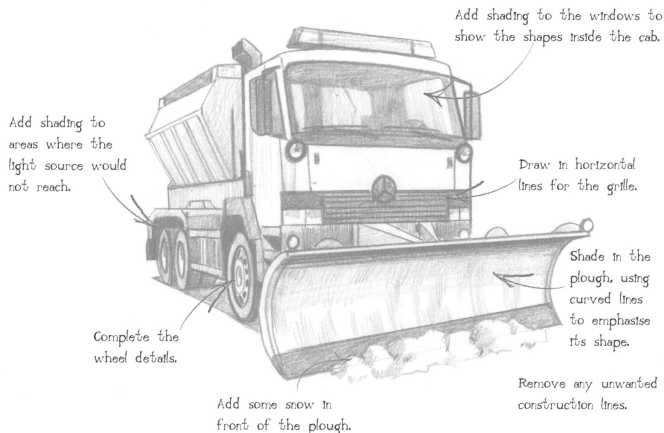

Draw in horizontal lines for the grille.

Shade in the plough, using curved lines to emphasise its shape.

Remove any unwanted construction lines.

Complete the wheel details.

Add some snow in front of the plough.

DRAW Tanker

Tankers often deliver dangerous fuels, liquids and powders. They have hazard warning signs on them to show what they contain.

Start your drawing with a three-dimensional rectangular box.

Allowing for perspective, draw in a vertical line marking roughly the first quarter of the box.

Lightly add two large ovals to show the ends of the tank.

Sketch in the angled shape of the cab using straight lines.

Draw in the wheel ellipses.

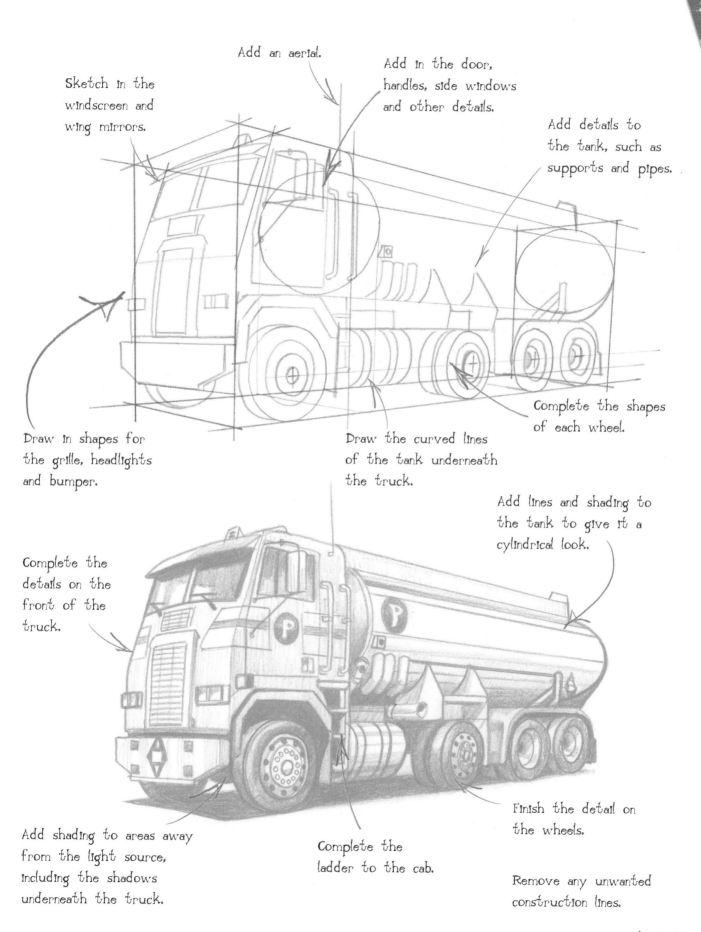

Add an aerial.

Sketch in the windscreen and wing mirrors.

Add in the door, handles, side windows and other details.

Add details to the tank, such as supports and pipes.

Draw in shapes for the grille, headlights and bumper.

Draw the curved lines of the tank underneath the truck.

Complete the shapes of each wheel.

Complete the details on the front of the truck.

Add lines and shading to the tank to give it a cylindrical look.

Add shading to areas away from the light source, including the shadows underneath the truck.

Complete the ladder to the cab.

Finish the detail on the wheels.

Remove any unwanted construction lines.

Future truck

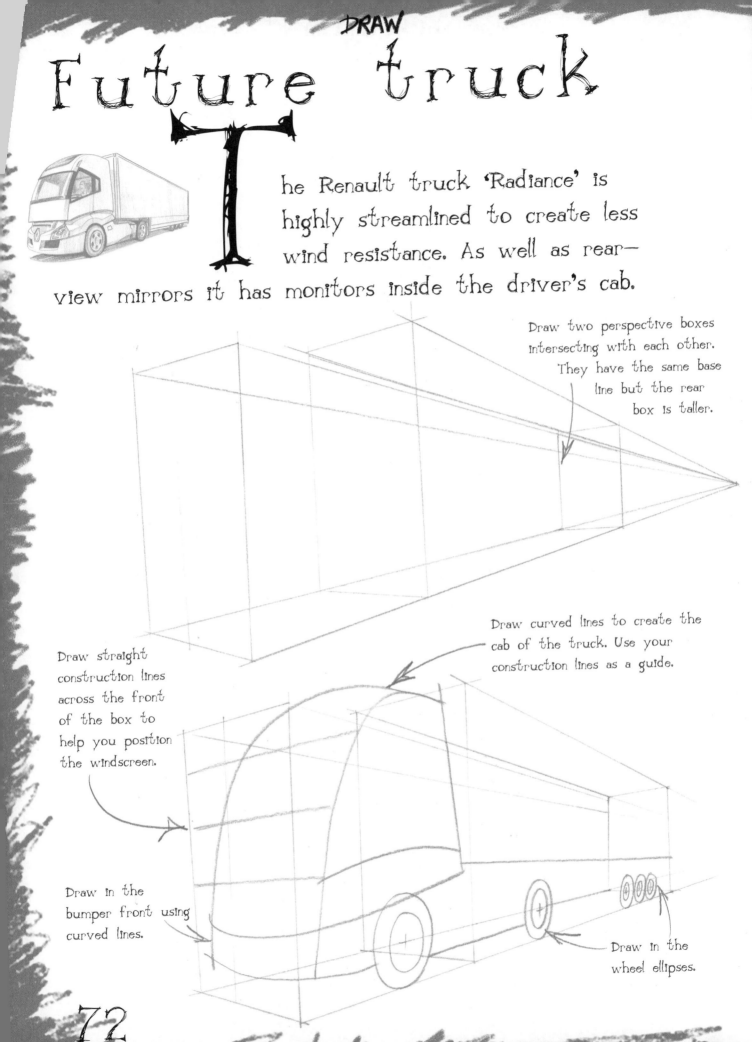

The Renault truck 'Radiance' is highly streamlined to create less wind resistance. As well as rear—view mirrors it has monitors inside the driver's cab.

Draw two perspective boxes intersecting with each other. They have the same base line but the rear box is taller.

Draw straight construction lines across the front of the box to help you position the windscreen.

Draw curved lines to create the cab of the truck. Use your construction lines as a guide.

Draw in the bumper front using curved lines.

Draw in the wheel ellipses.

Carefully position and
draw in the windscreen.

Draw in the box—
shaped trailer using
straight lines.

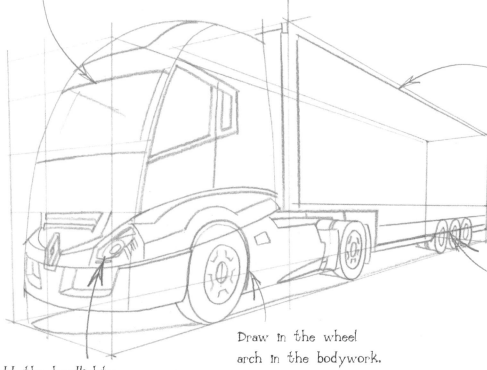

Add more detail to
the wheels; note that
they are partially
covered.

Draw in the wheel
arch in the bodywork.

Add the headlights
and other details.

Add the driver.

Use different tones
of shading for the
windscreen and the
inside of the cab.

Add shading to the
side of the trailer.

Complete the small
details on the wheels.

Add shading on
the front.

Add shading to areas that
face away from the light.

Remove any unwanted
construction lines.

73

Giant DRAW dump truck

These huge dump trucks work in opencast mines and quarries. They can carry 45 tonnes of rocks and dirt.

First draw a large box in perspective.

Add a central vertical line.

Draw in the large wheel ellipses.

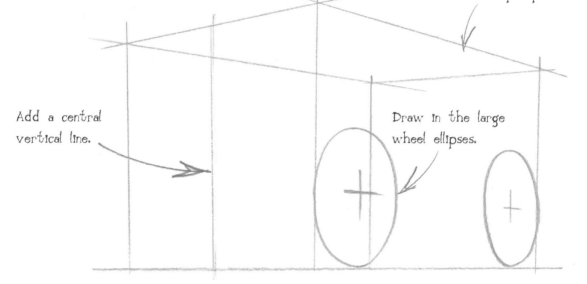

Use straight lines to draw in the area that overhangs the cab.

Use straight lines to construct the load space.

Add a box to the front of the truck.

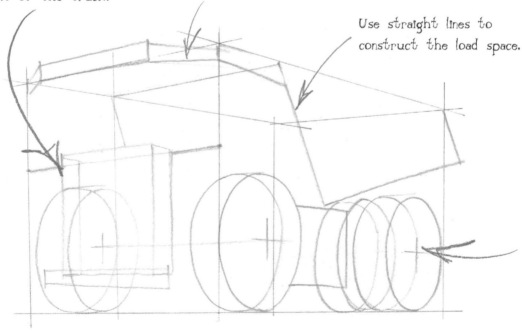

Construct the wheels with more ellipses.

74

Add detail to the overhanging part.

Sketch in the cab.

Draw in the ribs with straight lines.

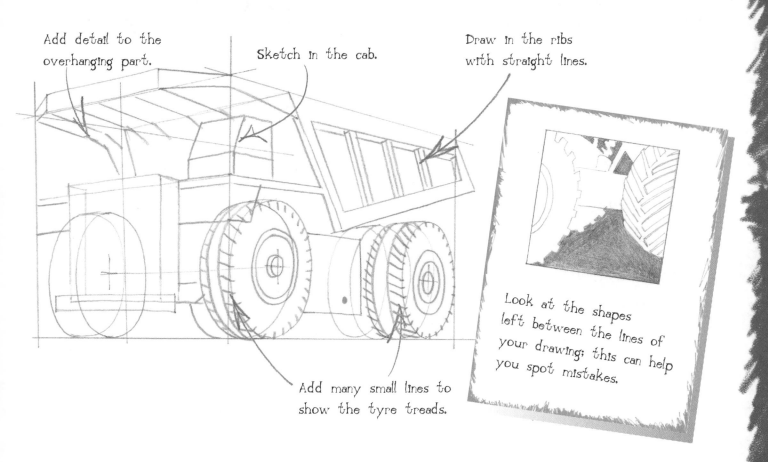

Look at the shapes left between the lines of your drawing; this can help you spot mistakes.

Add many small lines to show the tyre treads.

Add shading to areas where the light source will not reach.

Add some rubble at the top of the load space.

Draw in railings using straight lines.

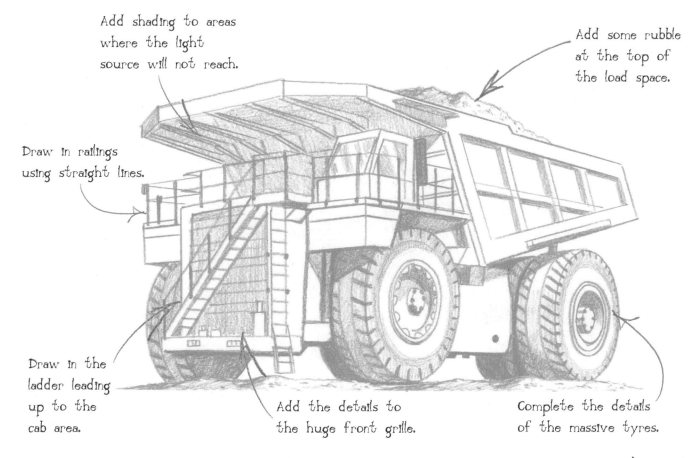

Draw in the ladder leading up to the cab area.

Add the details to the huge front grille.

Complete the details of the massive tyres.

Monster DRAW truck

As well as racing, these monster machines give spectacular shows of crushing cars and jumping.

They weigh around 4.5 tonnes and can squash a normal car with their giant wheels.

Draw two perspective boxes: one large box with a small one on top.

Draw in the body of the truck with a straight line.

Sketch in the basic shape of the monster truck's cabin.

Draw in the front of the truck. Use straight lines to position the grille and headlights.

Draw in the huge wheels with double ellipses. Join these using curved lines top and bottom.

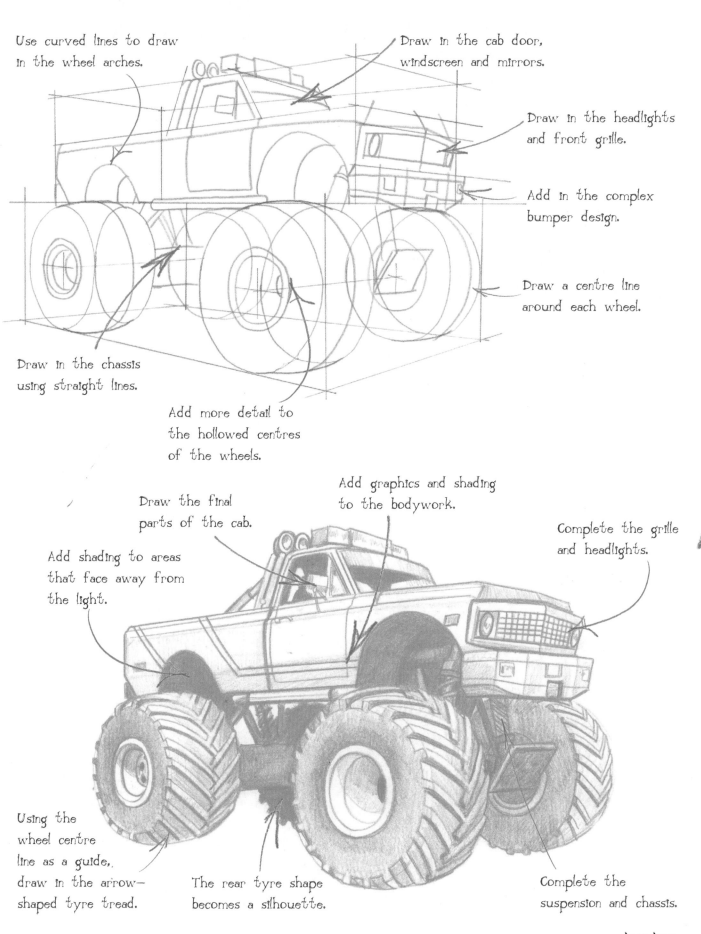

Use curved lines to draw in the wheel arches.

Draw in the cab door, windscreen and mirrors.

Draw in the headlights and front grille.

Add in the complex bumper design.

Draw a centre line around each wheel.

Draw in the chassis using straight lines.

Add more detail to the hollowed centres of the wheels.

Add graphics and shading to the bodywork.

Draw the final parts of the cab.

Complete the grille and headlights.

Add shading to areas that face away from the light.

Using the wheel centre line as a guide, draw in the arrow—shaped tyre tread.

The rear tyre shape becomes a silhouette.

Complete the suspension and chassis.

Freestyle BMX
DRAW

The BMX is the perfect bike for freestyling.

With pegs attached and a flexible setup, riders are capable of performing amazing tricks and stunts.

Start by drawing the rider as a simple stick figure with dots to indicate joints.

Add ovals for the head, body, hips and hands.

Draw simple triangles for the feet.

Using straight lines mark out the frame of the BMX.

Using the construction lines as a guide add tube shapes for the legs and circles for knees.

Sketch in the position of the facial features.

Using the construction lines as a guide, add tube shapes for the arms with circles for elbows.

Add more detail to the shape of the feet.

Add the BMX wheels to the bike frame.

Add parts of the frame and pegs.

Draw in the rider's
T-shirt.

Add some hair and a cap.

Sketch in basic shapes for
the hands and fingers.

Draw in the wheels using
construction lines to help
with perspective and scale.

Add shoes.

Sketch in the pedals.

Add the handle bars
using the construction
lines as a guide.

Add the main frame of the
bike using straight lines.

Finish the detail
of the head,
hat and hair.

Add detail and creases to
the trousers, especially
behind the knee.

Add dark tone to
areas where light
would not reach.

Add detail to
the shoes.

Finish the dark
metal handlebars.

Complete the wheels, adding dark
tone for the rubber tyres and
lines for the spokes.

Finish the frame of the
bike, adding a chain and
details to the pedals.
Add tone to suggest
tubular metal.

Remove any unwanted
construction lines.

DRAW
Skateboarding

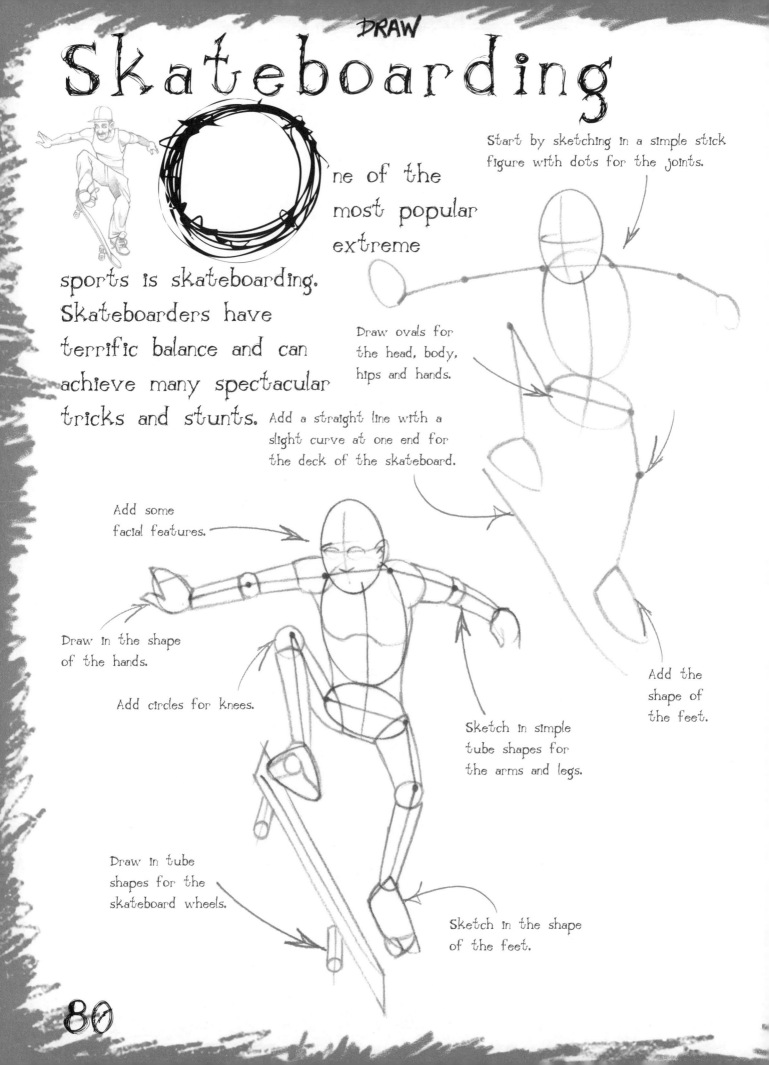

One of the most popular extreme sports is skateboarding. Skateboarders have terrific balance and can achieve many spectacular tricks and stunts.

Start by sketching in a simple stick figure with dots for the joints.

Draw ovals for the head, body, hips and hands.

Add a straight line with a slight curve at one end for the deck of the skateboard.

Add some facial features.

Draw in the shape of the hands.

Add circles for knees.

Sketch in simple tube shapes for the arms and legs.

Add the shape of the feet.

Draw in tube shapes for the skateboard wheels.

Sketch in the shape of the feet.

Draw in the fingers.

Add a cap to the head.

Draw in both arms using the construction lines as a guide. This arm is very foreshortened because of its angle.

Sketch in the trousers.

Add a vest.

Separate the tube into individual wheels.

Add muscle detail to the arms.

Complete the facial details.

Start to draw in the skateboarder's shoes.

Add dark tone to areas where light would not reach.

Shadows

Adding a shadow to your drawing can give it added drama. The shape of the skater's shadow will depend on the direction of the light source.

Add creases to the trouser fabric.

Finish drawing the skateboard.

Finish drawing the skateboard shoes, adding laces and detail.

Remove any unwanted construction lines.

81

DRAW
River rafting

River rafting is an extreme water sport. Each team will try to successfully navigate a rubber raft down fast flowing rivers and through rapids.

Sketch in five seated stick figures with dots for the joints.

Draw in a line between each figure's hands for the paddle handles.

Draw ovals for the heads, bodies and hands of all five figures.

Sketch in some curved lines to position the raft.

Add simple tube-shaped arms for each figure.

Add circles for elbows and knees.

Add the blades of the paddles.

Draw in simple tube-shaped legs.

Sketch in more of the upper raft using curved lines.

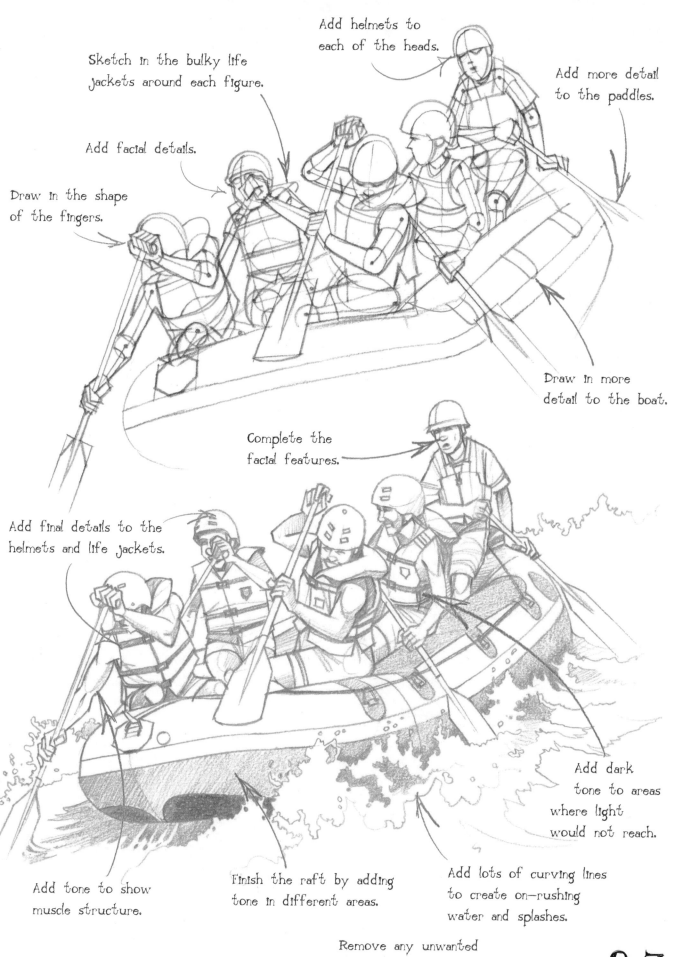

Add helmets to each of the heads.

Sketch in the bulky life jackets around each figure.

Add more detail to the paddles.

Add facial details.

Draw in the shape of the fingers.

Draw in more detail to the boat.

Complete the facial features.

Add final details to the helmets and life jackets.

Add dark tone to areas where light would not reach.

Add tone to show muscle structure.

Finish the raft by adding tone in different areas.

Add lots of curving lines to create on-rushing water and splashes.

Remove any unwanted construction lines.

83

DRAW ATV racing

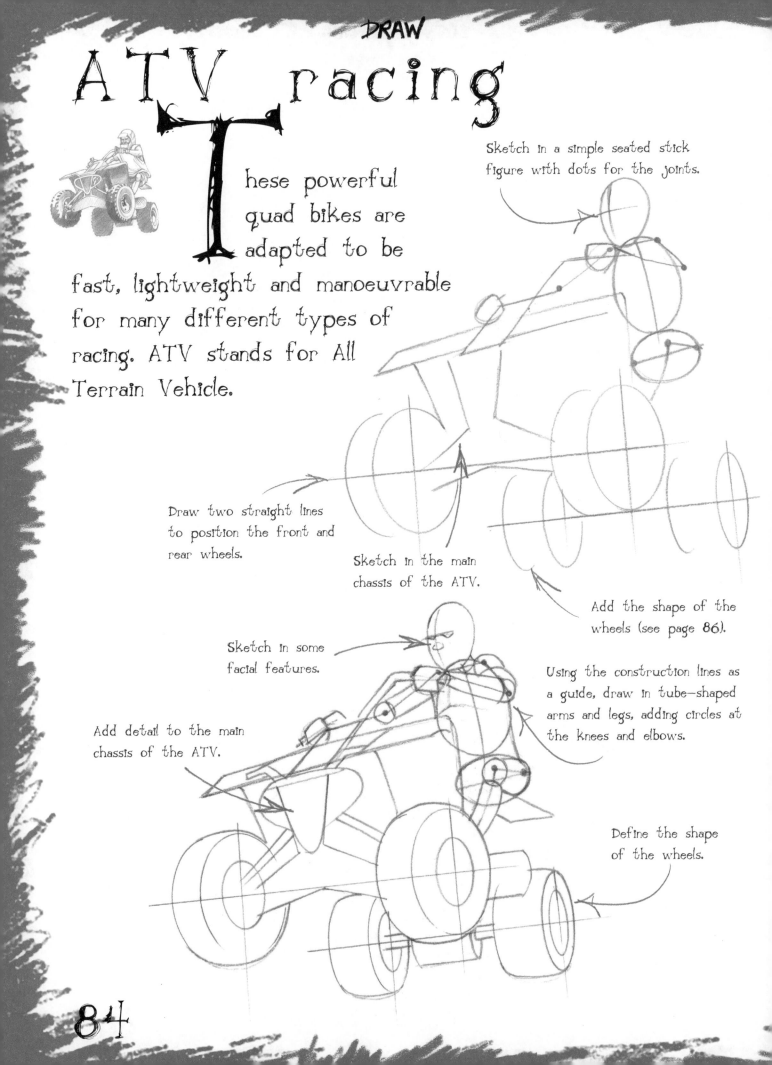

These powerful quad bikes are adapted to be fast, lightweight and manoeuvrable for many different types of racing. ATV stands for All Terrain Vehicle.

Sketch in a simple seated stick figure with dots for the joints.

Draw two straight lines to position the front and rear wheels.

Sketch in the main chassis of the ATV.

Add the shape of the wheels (see page 86).

Using the construction lines as a guide, draw in tube-shaped arms and legs, adding circles at the knees and elbows.

Sketch in some facial features.

Add detail to the main chassis of the ATV.

Define the shape of the wheels.

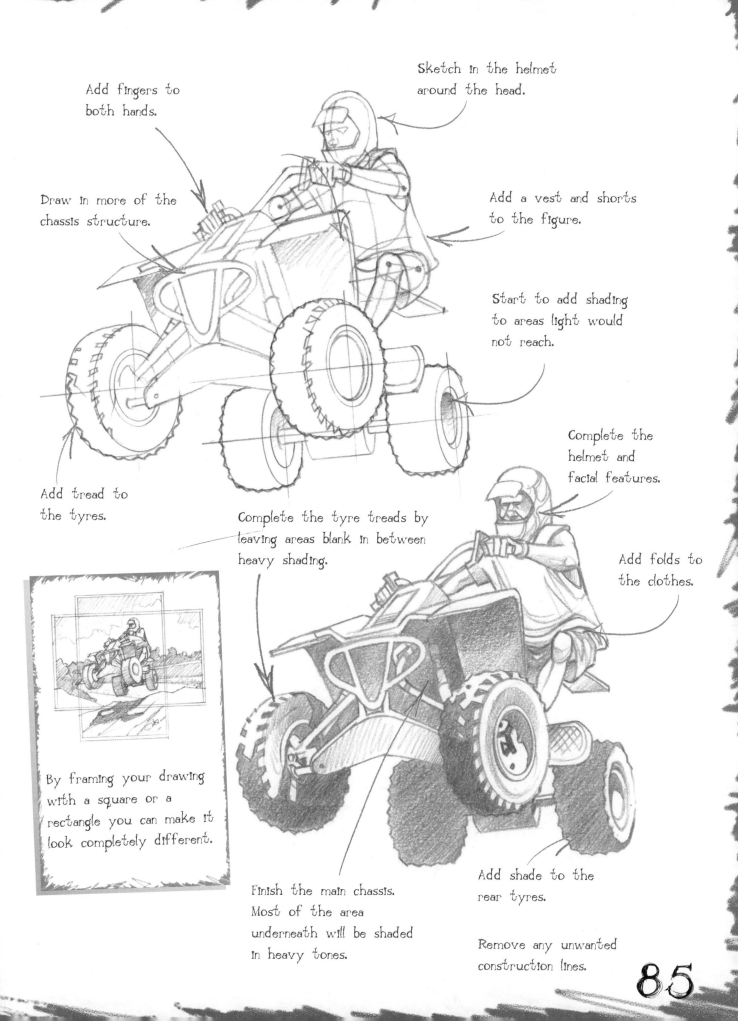

Sketch in the helmet around the head.

Add fingers to both hands.

Draw in more of the chassis structure.

Add a vest and shorts to the figure.

Start to add shading to areas light would not reach.

Add tread to the tyres.

Complete the helmet and facial features.

Complete the tyre treads by leaving areas blank in between heavy shading.

Add folds to the clothes.

By framing your drawing with a square or a rectangle you can make it look completely different.

Finish the main chassis. Most of the area underneath will be shaded in heavy tones.

Add shade to the rear tyres.

Remove any unwanted construction lines.

85

Wheels

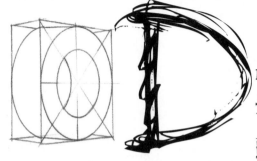

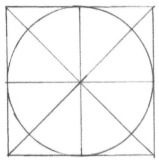

Drawing wheels from different perspectives can be tricky. The solution is to use construction lines to draw a square or perspective box, then fit the wheel within it.

Fit the circle in the box.

First draw a perspective box with vertical and horizontal lines running through the centre. Draw in the perimeter of the wheel, paying attention to the construction lines to make sure it touches at the edges of the perspective box, top, bottom, left and right. Add an inner ellipse for the inside of the wheel.

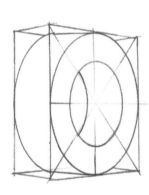

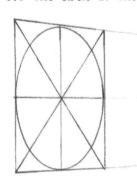

As the square turns into a perspective viewpoint, the circle becomes an ellipse.

Examples of different perspective wheels and the construction boxes needed:

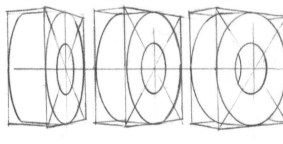
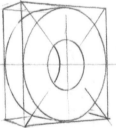
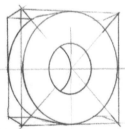
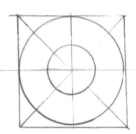

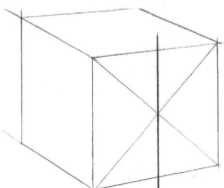

How to find the centre point.

To find the centre point of the perspective box, simply draw two lines from corner to corner. The point where they cross is the centre. Use this point to add your centre lines.

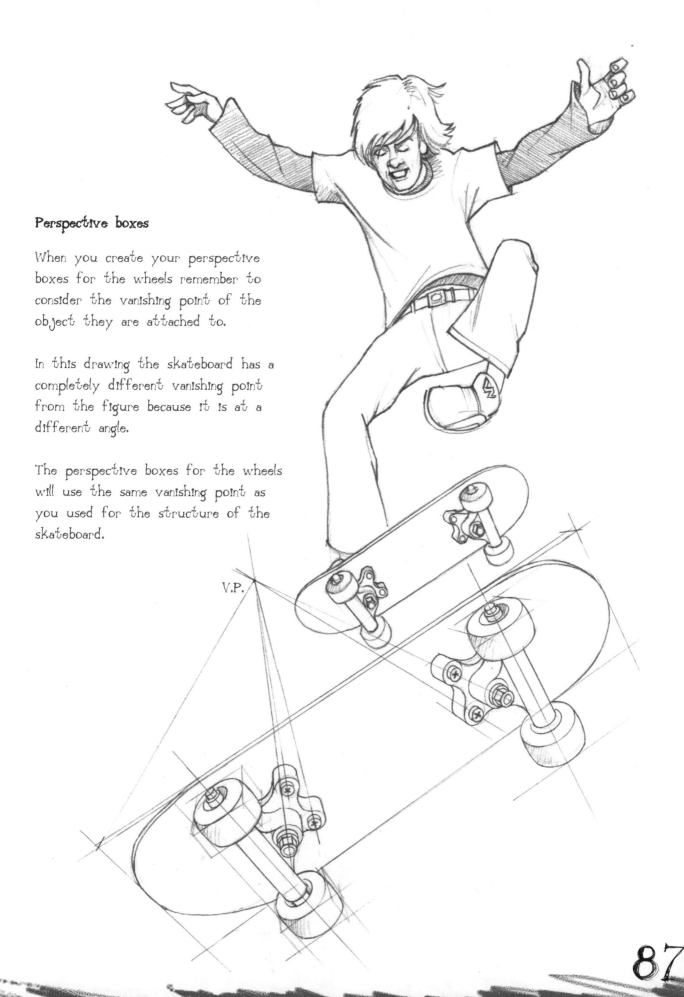

Perspective boxes

When you create your perspective boxes for the wheels remember to consider the vanishing point of the object they are attached to.

In this drawing the skateboard has a completely different vanishing point from the figure because it is at a different angle.

The perspective boxes for the wheels will use the same vanishing point as you used for the structure of the skateboard.

V.P.

Draw Wakeboarding

This extreme watersport involves being towed behind a boat at high speeds on a small wakeboard. Hitting the wake of the boat enables the wakeboarder to fly into the air and perform amazing tricks.

Draw ovals for the head, body and hands.

Add a line for the tow-rope handle.

Start by sketching in a simple stick figure with dots for the joints.

Add the shape of the feet.

Sketch in simple tube shapes for the arms.

Add some facial details.

Add circles for elbows.

Draw in the hand shapes.

Draw two parallel lines for the wakeboard.

Add more shape to the feet.

Draw in simple tube shapes for the legs, adding circles for knees.

Add curved windswept lines for hair.

Using the construction lines as a guide, add the curved shape of the arms.

Sketch in the tow rope.

Draw a vest on the figure.

Add fingers to the hands.

Draw a basic boot shape around the feet.

Add long baggy shorts.

Add tone to define muscle structure.

Finish the details of the tow rope and handle.

Complete the details of the head and hair.

Complete the shorts with a graphic design and creases.

Add folds and creases to the vest.

Finish the boot details.

Add the waves and splash of water.

Complete the wakeboard.

Remove any unwanted construction lines.

Spacecraft

DRAW

Space travellers use all sorts of unusual flying machines to move around space. Just like cars and planes today, they come in many different shapes and sizes.

Add a space traveller inside the cockpit of the spacecraft.

Start by drawing the basic shapes.

Draw two oval shapes joined together by a smaller rectangle.

Shade areas to make it appear three-dimensional.

Use bold, sweeping curves to the shapes to make it look futuristic.

Use perspective (see pages 8—9) to make the craft look as though it is hurtling through space.

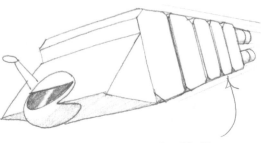

Round off the corners of the shapes.

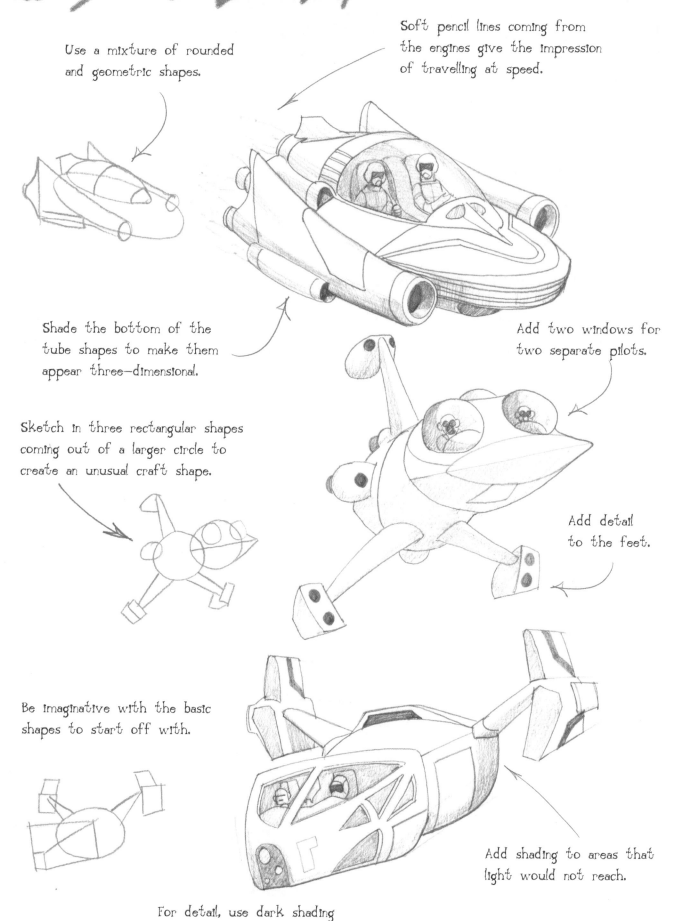

Use a mixture of rounded and geometric shapes.

Soft pencil lines coming from the engines give the impression of travelling at speed.

Shade the bottom of the tube shapes to make them appear three-dimensional.

Add two windows for two separate pilots.

Sketch in three rectangular shapes coming out of a larger circle to create an unusual craft shape.

Add detail to the feet.

Be imaginative with the basic shapes to start off with.

Add shading to areas that light would not reach.

For detail, use dark shading to indicate any areas in the bodywork that go inward.

Space vehicles DRAW

People in space drive various types of vehicles to jet between planets and travel around the galaxy. Some are designed for speed, some for comfort and some even for combat.

For this space scooter, start by sketching a large oval shape with a triangle at the front.

Add curved lines and rounded shapes for the detail of the vehicle.

Draw an oval for the head, with helmet detail.

Add tube shapes for limbs.

Draw circles for the joints.

Sketch triangle shapes on the front of the machine.

Shade the front of the vehicle to look like glass.

Complete the detail of the driver by shading in the helmet and making his suit look futuristic.

Shade in the areas where light would not reach.

Remove any unwanted construction lines.

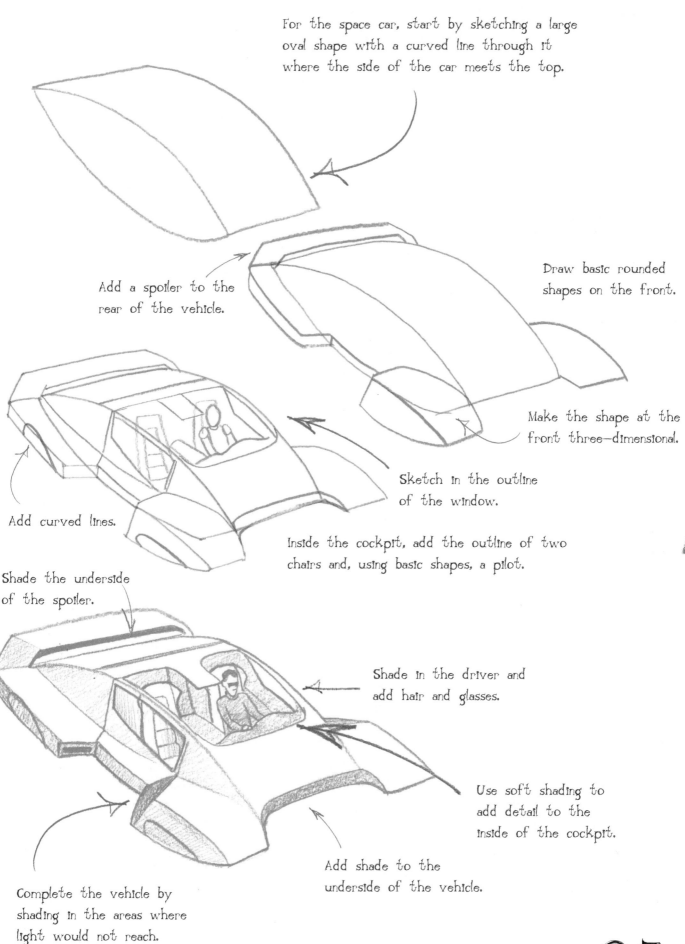

For the space car, start by sketching a large oval shape with a curved line through it where the side of the car meets the top.

Add a spoiler to the rear of the vehicle.

Draw basic rounded shapes on the front.

Make the shape at the front three-dimensional.

Sketch in the outline of the window.

Add curved lines.

Inside the cockpit, add the outline of two chairs and, using basic shapes, a pilot.

Shade the underside of the spoiler.

Shade in the driver and add hair and glasses.

Use soft shading to add detail to the inside of the cockpit.

Add shade to the underside of the vehicle.

Complete the vehicle by shading in the areas where light would not reach.

93

Glossary

Chiaroscuro The practice of drawing high-contrast pictures with a lot of black and white, but not much grey.

Composition The arrangement of the parts of a picture on the drawing paper.

Construction lines Guidelines used in the early stages of a drawing. They are usually erased later.

Fixative A type of resin used to spray over a finished drawing to prevent smudging. **It should only be used by an adult.**

Focal point A central point of interest.

Foreshortening Drawing part of a figure shorter than it really is, so it looks as though it is pointing towards the viewer.

Light source The direction from which the light seems to come in a drawing.

Perspective A method of drawing in which near objects are shown larger than faraway objects to give an impression of depth.

Pose The position assumed by a figure.

Proportion The correct relationship of scale between each part of the drawing.

Silhouette A drawing that shows only a flat, dark shape, like a shadow.

Three-dimensional Having an effect of depth, so as to look lifelike or real.

Vanishing point The place in a perspective drawing where parallel lines appear to meet.

Index

A
Airbus A380 42—43
articulated truck 64—65
Aston Martin DBS 12—13
ATV 84—85

B
backgrounds 17, 28, 45
Bentley Speed 20—21
'Blackbird' 36—37
BMX 78—79
bow 48, 50—51, 52, 54—55, 56, 58
bowsprit 60

C
charcoal 6
composition 13, 38, 49, 61, 67, 85
Concorde 38—39
construction lines 8—9, 15, 21, 24—25, 29, 31, 33, 35, 37, 39, 41, 43, 45, 47, 49, 51, 53, 55, 57, 59, 62—63, 65, 67, 69, 71, 72—73, 86
crayons 6

D
drawing tools 6—7

E
ellipses 10, 14—15, 16, 18, 21, 22, 26, 31, 42, 62, 64, 68, 70, 72, 74, 76
exhaust pipes 65, 69

F
F16-A Fighting Falcon 40—41
felt-tips 6—7
Ferrari F1 24—25
Ferrari FXX 22—23
fire engine 78—79
fishing boat 56—57
fixative 6
flags 61

Ford GT 14—15
future truck 72—73

G
giant dump truck
    74—75

H
hats 79, 81
headlights 63, 65, 67,
    69, 71, 73, 77
helmet 83, 85
Honda Civic R 10—11
horizon 8

J
Jolly Roger 61

L
light and shade 13, 15, 21,
    23, 25, 47, 49, 51, 53,
    55, 59, 63, 65, 67, 69,
    71, 73, 75, 77
Lockheed SR-71 (see
    'Blackbird')

M
mast 48, 52, 60
materials 6—7
mirrors 35, 47, 68
Mitchell, R.J. 33
monster truck
    76—77

N
NASCAR 18—19
negative space 75

P
pastels 6
perspective 8—9, 10—11,
    12, 14, 16, 18, 20, 22, 24,
    26, 44, 58, 60, 61, 62,
    64, 68, 72, 74, 76,
    86—87, 90
Pitts, Curtis 34
Pitts Special 34—35

Q
quad bikes 84—85

R
racing truck 66—67
racing yacht 48—49
Richthofen, Baron von (The
    Red Baron) 28—29
river rafting 82—83
rowing boat 50—51

S
sails 49, 53, 61
Schneider Trophy 32
schooner 52
shadows 81
silhouette 77
skateboard 80—81, 87
Sopwith triplane 28
space car 93
spacecraft 90—91
space scooter 92
Space Ship One 44—45
speedboat 46—47
Subaru Impreza 16—17
Supermarine S6B 32—33
Supermarine Spitfire
    30—31

T
tanker 70—71
three-dimensional
    (drawings) 10—11, 13, 17,
    25, 27, 32, 46, 50, 55,
    56, 70, 90—91, 93
Thrust SSC 26—27
topsail schooner 52—53

V
vanishing point 8—9, 60,
    87

W
wakeboarding 88—89
water sports 82—83,
    88—89,
waves 49, 53, 55, 59
weapons 61
wheels 78—79, 80—81,
    84—85,

Y
yacht 48—49

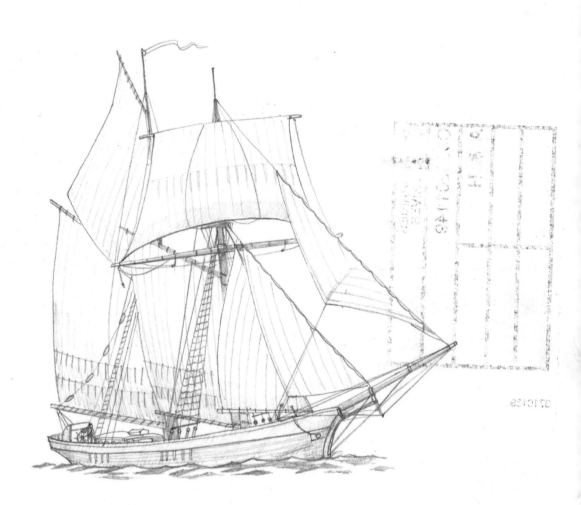